# Robes of Silk, Feet of Clay

The true story of a love affair with
Maharishi Mahesh Yogi, the creator of the
Transcendental Meditation movement

by

*Judith Bourque*

Waterside Press

Robes of Silk, Feet of Clay
Author: Judith Bourque
Copyright © 2018 by Judith Bourque
www.robesofsilkfeetofclay.com

Pictures: Pages 26—29 ©Adrian Stähli, pages 91, 249 © Jonathan Miller, pages 118—119 ©Theo Fehr, page 172 ©Eric Berndt, pages 226—268, page 279 ©Judith Bourque, Jean Paul Klijntunte, Maciej Komosinski, Hans Nirholt, Francesca Pinoni, Niklas Schaper, Melanie Tchacos, page 275 ©PeO Larsson. Remaining photos belong to the author's private archive.

Printed in Estonia by Printing Partners Group
Third printing 2018
Cover and Graphic form: Mia Raunegger, design4u2.se
ISBN-13: 978-1-947637-80-1 print edition
ISBN-13: 978-1-947637-81-8 ebook edition

Waterside Press
2055 Oxford Avenue
Cardiff, Ca 92007
www.waterside.com

"*There are two ways to be.
One is at war with reality,
and the other is at peace.*"

-*Byron Katie*-

## Acknowledgements

Thanks first of all to Dr. Rob McCutchan. "Robes of Silk, Feet of Clay" is actually the title of a book that he was going to write in 1976 when all the pieces of the puzzle finally came together for him, and he was certain that his guru had broken his vows. In the end, he changed his mind and decided not to write it. When I came across his title and read it for the first time, I knew that those six words contained the essence of what I had experienced. He has kindly given me use of it for my book.

Thanks to David Sieveking, whose film "David Wants to Fly" nudged me out of hibernation.

Thanks also to Conny Larsson, who has a special understanding of my life experience. He also had a hidden relationship with an internationally known guru, Sathya Sai Baba, and has "come out" by writing a book on the subject.

Thanks to Adrian Stähli for the use of his photos from Maharishi's funeral.

Thanks to Mia Raunegger for her exceptional layout and cover design.

Thanks to Indcen Travel, Stockholm. This company has over twenty years of experience in organizing trips to India and skillfully tailored a journey that enabled us to walk in the footsteps of the divine masters.

Thanks to members of my "soul family" who gave feedback and support along the way: Caren, Grace, Jonathan, Lena, Michelle, Susan, Daniel, and many others.

Thanks to Jean Paul Klijntunte, Joe Harley, Rob van Beek, and Brian Wagner for their special support.

Thanks to those who supported this project financially, who wish to remain anonymous.

And thanks to my Higher Self for getting me through the storm.

*This book is dedicated to*

*My son Jonathan, and*
*My grandchildren, Lucia and Amos*

# Contents

Some of the names have been changed to protect the identity
of the persons involved.

# Foreword

Judith Bourque has written an extraordinary book, and this edition is a continuation of her extraordinary story. However, the extraordinary nature of this book is quite different than what most would think. I initially heard about the first edition in the social media frequented by current and former "TMer's" several months before it was published. It was said that the book was about a woman's intimate relationship with Maharishi written by the woman herself. As someone who was deeply involved with the Transcendental Meditation movement for many decades and as a clinical psychologist I thought, "This will be interesting." And interesting it was, not only for me personally, but also for the impact it had on the greater TM community.

The reaction to Robes of Silk Feet of Clay was quite predictable. People who had soured in their relationship with the TM movement and Maharishi simply saw the book as a confirmation of what they already believed: that Maharishi was a fraud. The other reaction from those still deeply invested in the TM movement was that the book was a fraud. The author was either lying or actually delusional in some manner with the prevailing assumption that what she reported simply could not have happened. These reactions, of course, are to be expected. It is what psychologists refer to as cognitive dissonance. Two or more beliefs are mutually exclusive of one another, yet both are held by the mind simultaneously. Maharishi cannot be both one of the greatest spiritual masters to walk the earth and also duplicitous regarding his relationship with women. Spiritual masters are not duplicitous. Duplicitous people are not spiritual masters. He must be one or the other. So with this, people resolve their dissonance by "adjusting" their underlying relationship to one of the perspectives, which results in utterly dismissing the opposite perspective. And life goes on just as before.

But I want to suggest another perspective, another understanding that moves beyond these pairs of opposites. What if both are true? I say this because of my own experience with Maharishi. I have had profound spiritual experiences over the past 42 years triggered by Maharishi's presence and by the practice of his TM and TM Sidhis Program. So, I certainly cannot dismiss Maharishi as some sort of spiritual fraud. But I also cannot deny others' experiences, and my own to a lesser degree, of Maharishi's more prosaic personality traits. So how do we move beyond this apparent paradox?

One way is through the Vedantic concept of lesh-avidya which translates as the "remains of ignorance." This concept states that regardless of the degree of one's enlightenment there is always a small degree of dross or limitation due to the innate nature of the mind and body. So even the most enlightened saint has a tiny degree of ignorance as long as the body is there.

Another way of understanding Maharishi comes from the Tripura Rahasya[1] and its discussion of different types of Jnanis (enlightened persons). All have equal degrees of realization, but their minds function in different ways, "… and thus you find among them some highly irritable, some lustful and others pious and dutiful and so on."

But I believe there is another way to move beyond the paradox of Maharishi and that is to simply let go. All our judgments regarding anything are of the individual mind. The mind seeks pleasure and avoids pain based upon its limited nature. That which produces pleasure is "good" and that which causes pain is "bad." To follow this judgment of the mind leads to deeper and deeper bondage. So we move beyond this bondage of the mind by simultaneously allowing all experiences to

---

1  Tripura Rahasya or The Mystery Beyond the Trinity, Tamil Nadu, India: V.S. Ramanan, 2008 p. 197. (The Tripura Rahasya is an ancient sanskrit classic on the subject of Vedantic metaphysics.)

simply be as they are. Our mind will fight this and attempt to organize experience into a network of mutually supportive concepts. These concepts are an egoic delusion. To drop these concepts created by judgments is to say, "I don't know." Not an "I don't know" of ignorance, but an "I don't know" of wisdom.

This dropping of concepts is what Judith's book offers to the discriminating reader. It is an advanced technique that will move you beyond the pairs of opposites and paradoxically closer to Maharishi.

Peter L. Sutphen, Psy.D.                    *December 18, 2014*
Coconut Creek, Florida

# Preface

This book is the story of a love affair kept secret, a secret I really thought would follow me to my grave or to my ashes, whichever way I leave. I was sure that the whole experience was behind me, that I had digested it, and if not completely understood it that I could comfortably just leave it alone, the past not being that interesting to me anymore. It was the now that was important.

And yet, here we are 180 degrees in the opposite direction.

It all started because of a dream...not a dream of wishes and hopes, but a dream during sleep where the man whom I had loved in my youth came to me with a message. His name was Maharishi Mahesh Yogi, a spiritual teacher who was a guru for the Beatles, Clint Eastwood, David Lynch, Deepak Chopra, Donovan, Jerry Seinfeld, Mia Farrow, Mike Love, Paul Horn and a whole slew of other well-known personalities as well as for 6.000.000 meditators spread out across the globe.

Three years passed before I understood the message in my dream fully. During that time Maharishi had died and been cremated on the banks of the River Ganges, his ashes thrown into her holy waters.

What happened next was that a German film-maker, David Sieveking, having heard rumors about Maharishi breaking his vows in secrecy, succeeded in finding me. Maharishi's teachings had touched David Sieveking's life through his admiration for meditating film director David Lynch, and that contact led him on a spiritual journey documented in the film he was making.

It was not until David, with polite persistence, convinced me that his approach in the documentary would be one of balance, neither total condemnation of Maharishi nor fanatical idealization, did I start even to consider speaking publicly of this matter.

David's request made me start to waver, but I was still very unsure. After all, I had been silent for the entirety of my adult life to the point where the silence had simply become a part of who I was, or who I thought I was. Even though Maharishi had died, the thought of actually telling my story was still very upsetting and very confusing. In the hopes of finding some clarity, I booked a channeled session with a spiritual counselor, and it was this session that helped me to fully understand the message in my dream.

Yes, it *was* time to take the relationship out of the closet. It wasn't just perhaps a good thing to do…it was in fact the right thing to do, not only for myself but for Maharishi as well. The details of that session are written down further on in the text, but for now I will say that when I finally took up my pen to share my story with you, I no longer felt afraid or uncertain.

# Preface to the Third Edition

This is the third edition of Robes of Silk Feet of Clay. The first part of the book has been polished; I've corrected some facts, shortened here, lengthened there, and added photos that have come out of hiding since I first wrote the book. There is an epilogue describing some of the reactions I've received during the years that have passed, as well as a description of my journey back to Rishikesh and Maharishi's ashram during the winter of 2014 and again in 2017.

And yes, a small request: since the first edition I have learned that many skip the chapters about my childhood, eager to get into the story of what happened with Maharishi. Please start at the beginning of the book, since these chapters reveal the conditioning that helped create a willingness to surrender my heart, my body, and my mind to a guru.

I would also like to add that my experience with Maharishi has in no way diminished my love of India and its culture. The phenomena of following a charismatic, religious leader beyond reasonable limits can be found within all the major world religions, as well as within business and politics. That manner of relating to each other no longer serves us. Did it ever?

DAVID WANTS TO FLY
EIN YOGISCHES ABENTEUER

EIN FILM VON DAVID SIEVEKING

Berlinale

60.
Internationale
Filmfestspiele
Berlin 11.–21.02.10

Berlinale Palast

# Maharishi and me? At the Berlin Film Festival?

"Oh God, I'm late. I can't be late! I even left *early* so I wouldn't be late! Where's the movie theater? Oh my God, this is the wrong movie theater..."

Ms Spaghetti...that's what my energy feels like in trying to fit into to a societal time line. In Sweden, where I live now, being on time is a cultural virtue. Sometimes clients will come late to a booked appointment with their hearts in their throats, panting and sweating. I always tell them how much I love it when they are late, since I am always late myself. But they still don't believe me, and keep on excusing themselves as they take their coats off.

On the second try, I found my way to the correct movie theater where David Sieveking's film "David Wants to Fly" would have its premiere at the Berlin Film Festival and started wading through the crowd. Thankfully one of the producers recognized me in the throng of people waiting outside to get in to see the first film of the documentary section, and led me down to the very front row of a large salon that seats about 500. He said that I would be introduced at the end of the film, and that was why he wanted me to sit there. David came up to me and said that he would like to tell the public I was there after the showing, but wanted to check first if that was ok. My answer came out easily... "Sure, David. I'm ready."

This was the very first time I would see the production in its entirety. I had been allowed to approve the final edit of my interview which became the deciding factor for giving an interview about my love affair with Maharishi to David and his producers, but had only relied on David's intention regarding the rest of the film. I really had no idea of what I had gotten myself into.

The very first pictures and the very first sounds set the stage for a film with spiritual content. Since I work as a filmmaker and editor myself, I expected to be overly critical, but fell easily into the journey David's film took his public on. First awe, then curious, then funny. Curious again, oops, pain. Remember, remember, oh, more pain. Then joy. Then embarrassed. It was a bumpy ride.

The best part was being taken to places and people

I had been curious about for decades but chosen not to go to. David had worked on it for nearly five years so rest assured he had put his heart, soul and pocketbook into the birth of this child. The film was professionally done—direction, photography, sound, edit. I found myself reacting to it as a colleague on the one hand, and as a private person on the other.

I saw and listened to David Lynch, whose innocence and devotion to Maharishi reminded me of my own, before the bubble burst.

I got to see the inner workings of the TM Movement in recent years, complete with wealthy Western men dressed in white robes and little gold crowns that Maharishi established during the latter part of his life.

I witnessed Maharishi's funeral in India. 40,000 followers had gone to Allahabad to witness his cremation. I felt a wave of emotion as his ashes were released into the Ganges River, with rose petals raining down from a helicopter flying overhead.

I watched brain waves on machines as David was plugged in to be measured while he meditated. He looked funny with the red wired helmet on.

I saw my wrinkles on the screen in 35mm HD projection from the front row.

I heard snickers at my apparel and thought, "Yes, I look like a middle-aged hippy," regretting that I had not changed clothes for the interview. The shooting was done during a course in Shamanic journeying that I had been teaching in Germany.

I visited Guru Dev's Ashram high in the Himalayas, and met the presiding Shankaracharya of Jyotir Math, who knew Maharishi as a young man at the same Ashram. I didn't expect that he would have much positive to say, and he didn't either. There is a tremendous amount of jealousy and competition within the Hindu culture between the various gurus and their movements.

When the showing was over, I found myself being applauded by hundreds of people after David introduced me as having the courage to speak my truth, but for a few seconds it felt like they were applauding me for being Maharishi's lover. After having been in hiding since 1972 on that subject, this was quite a "life doesn't turn out the way we expect" moment.

During the premiere dinner, Sieveking and I had a few moments to talk about my reactions to his film.

"David, what I am feeling is double. On the one hand, I think your film is very well done as a film, and then as a person, with my history, it is more critical than I had expected."

"It is more critical than I expected too," he said. "But when Lynch and the TM movement started working against me, it just developed that way."

I found myself sitting there, expecting to feel more upset with David.

"And yet somehow I don't feel that you tricked me. Everything in your film is true...I think it's just that there are a lot of other aspects that are not said, aspects of positive things that are missing in the film. I'm afraid that no one will ever want to learn to meditate after seeing this film, and I still teach meditation!"

"I don't think my film is negative about meditation in general...but I would rather motivate people to em-

24

bark on their spiritual journey by finding their own way. I think it is misleading to claim that one special technique is the highway to enlightenment," David countered.

We left it at that. Earlier he had said that he wanted to keep on working on the film, and that was a point of view I could understand. How could he ever be "finished" with this subject?

After the first showing, someone in the audience raised her hand and said that in the future she would like to see Sieveking's "David Wants to Fly" and David Lynch's coming documentary on the life of Maharishi at the same showing. I would hope that can manifest, followed of course by an open discussion. It might turn out that it will be the resulting dialogue around these films which will hold the seed of truth about what Transcendental Meditation is and what it isn't, who Maharishi was and who he wasn't.

I saw David's film three times during the festival and continued to move through a psychic blender of mixed emotions. Many came up to me afterwards to express personal reactions.

Almost all were positive, including a woman whose brother had become one of the "Rajas" around Maharishi and who had died recently. She thanked me for speaking out, and said she felt that he was never supported or encouraged by the movement to look after his health properly and that he would have lived longer and been happier if he had not been so deeply involved. She described him as being very emotionally dependent upon Maharishi's moods.

I got to experience Maharishi's funeral in India through David Sieveking's film, "David Wants to Fly".

Maharishi's body on display before cremation.

40000 followers came to Allahabad, India to participate in
Maharishi's funeral.

Collecting the ashes.  *© Adrian Stähli*

**Maharishi Mahesh Yogi's ashes being released into Mother Ganges.**

One couple stood in front of me, holding out their tickets with a pen and speaking German. I just stood there looking like a question mark and hadn't a clue as to what they wanted. The producer had to tell me what to do..."Judith, they want your autograph." Feeling like a complete nitwit, I quickly signed their tickets.

Another person sought me out outside the theater. First he needed to know whether or not what I had implied about my relationship with Maharishi in the film was true, down to the letter.

I told him it was. He looked as though he just had to swallow some bad tasting medicine.

"Are you surprised?" I asked.

"I'm surprised at you. It's so personal..."

"I'm not doing this to hurt Maharishi," I said.

"But you did," he replied. "I have been meditating for 32 years..."

He was obviously a devout practitioner of Transcendental Meditation.

I went on.

"You see, when Maharishi asked me to promise not to tell anyone about our relationship, he brought me into his lie. I've had to live that lie all these years. What I have found out is that I needed to let myself out of the prison of having to cover for him."

"So you are doing this for your own sake?" he asked.

"Yes, very much so. And by the way, Maharishi came to me in a dream and asked me to 'take him out of the closet.' It is my understanding that he felt he had left some bad karma behind him by dying without telling the truth and that he wanted help with that situation. So I believe that I am actually assisting him to clean it up."

He and the young woman he was with listened, but we parted on that note. Even though he was upset with me, I was still grateful, seeing our conversation as preparation for reactions that I would undoubtedly meet when this book was released. And he may have seen the karma aspect as my own construct, but the concept of karma has now become a part of my world view, even though I was not raised with this belief system.

I came away from the Berlin Film Festival rather shocked at feeling so much lighter after "coming out" and was genuinely surprised at how deeply having to live a lie has affected me. I had talked myself into believing that I didn't care anymore. It seems that we humans have an amazing ability to adjust to life's circumstances, but there is a big difference between coping and flourishing.

I also felt grateful that David and his producers had provided me with an opportunity to share my experience. As for the film as a whole, I left with a feeling of having witnessed a tragedy...the tragedy of how a man who was the carrier of such truth had allowed himself and his divine intention to be swayed by human attachments to the degree that many of his teachings would become seriously questioned.

# Pappa
# is in Heaven

My cousin Jimmy and I sat on the front step of our house. We were just kids...I was six years old, and he was eight. He was more of a brother to me than my own brother who was four years older than I was, and most of the time just wanted me to move to another planet.

"I hope Pappa doesn't die." I said.

"Me too," said Jimmy.

We must have been aware that my grandfather was very sick. My cousin had been sent to spend the night at our house, instead of sleeping at his own home which was shared with my maternal grandparents.

"Pappa" was what we called our grandfather.

Here I'm 3 years old, outside my grandparents' country home in Princeton, Massachusetts.

Americans usually call their grandparents Grampa and Gramma, but this side of our family was from Finland, and we retained some of the cultural traditions from Northern Europe in our family. My mother was born in the United States, yet her first language was Finnish, and my grandfather spoke English with a heavy accent in spite of having lived in the United States for more than forty years.

Pappa was our hero. If one were to judge from his exterior, there would be no logical explanation for his status amongst us four children (my brother and myself, and my two cousins, who were also brother and sister). It seemed as though he mostly sat on the front porch of my grandparents' farm, reading the newspaper and smoking his pipe in a large, wicker chair with a worn, cloth cushion. Pappa had severe arthritis and was so crippled by it that he could only get around very slowly with the support of his crutches.

What was so special about Pappa? I don't really know...maybe it was that he loved children. He cared about us, and we could feel it. And, most likely due to his age and his illness, he also had the time to be with us. Or rather we would be with him since he could hardly run around and chase us in the fields on their land. A lot of the time we just played on the lawn of the farmhouse, knowing that he sat behind us in his chair. I suppose he was our babysitter while the women were inside preparing meals, cleaning and doing the laundry. Sometimes he'd peel an apple for us. He would peel it slowly, slowly, without breaking the peel as it gradually wound itself down onto the porch floor. And we would watch in suspense to see whether or not he could do it again and manage to keep the peel in one unbroken spiral. But he always did, and then gave us the apple to gobble up.

Other times he'd make us acorn pipes, carving out the center of an acorn and making a small hole on the side in order to stick in a match and make it look like a tobacco pipe. This was in the days before everyone knew that smoking was not good for your health, so we could walk around with the pipes stuck in our mouths acting grown-up without anybody getting on our case. I also remember sitting on his knee as he read a children's book to me with such a heavy dialect that I couldn't wholly understand what he was saying. It was a story about a little duck that got all wet in a puddle, and he laughed when the duck got all wet. So I laughed when he laughed, wanting him to think that I could understand what he was saying.

But more important than the quiet, peaceful memories of lovely summer days was that Pappa represented complete and utter safety. In this very same farmhouse in a small, New England country town lived my grandmother, or "Mummo" as we called her. Mummo was considerably more nervous than my grandfather. She was always fretting about something.

A memory etched into my inner child's mind is how she one day threatened to go get "the belt" and beat me with it. The sin to be punished was that I had been climbing in apple trees with my cousin Jimmy and eating green apples. This, she was sure, would give me a terrible stomach ache. I remember standing beside my grandfather, who was sitting on his indoor chair in the kitchen, clinging to his pant leg in fear. I can't remember what he said…perhaps he spoke to my grandmother in Finnish. All I know is that he prevented me from getting beaten, and I stayed glued to his side until the danger was over. My mother told me in later years that my grandfather had a very special relationship to children and that he used to say, "There will be no beatings in this house." She said that Pappa was of the opinion that one should never even raise one's voice to a child.

Just knowing that Pappa was there, sitting in his chair on the porch, gave me a feeling of safety.

I still wish that I had had the opportunity to get to know my grandfather when I was an adult. He was the one responsible for bringing my mother's side of the family to the United States. According to Mom, he and my grandmother had been living and working in Russia when it became evident that Pappa would be forced to join the Cossacks and go to war for the Russian Czar. At that point, he told his family that he was not going to fight any man's war. He and a friend bought a first-class ocean liner ticket to Canada and came over the border to the United States from that direction.

He sent for his wife Mary and stepdaughter Helen to come later, which they did and then fathered three children of his own at the beginning of the 19th century in Fitchburg, Massachusetts. Their first child, a boy, died as an infant which may explain my grandfather's special attitude toward children. My mother told me that she used to see him holding her brother's baby shoes in his hands from time to time and that he would smell them.

Suddenly, one day, he was just gone.

I remember asking my aunt where Pappa was. My aunt's home was the equivalent of day care for me since my mother was working full time as an elementary school teacher. Mummo and Pappa were a part of my everyday routine.

My aunt bent down to talk to me at my level. Her voice became softer and lower as she said gently, "Pappa is in heaven now."

That was it. I don't remember any more talking

about my grandfather's death. I do remember going to a place where there was a lot of grass and looking at some big stone with letters on it, but none of that really meant anything to me as a child. It was just a thing grown-ups decided that I had to do.

Many years later, I was in the state of Washington, training to become a teacher of Re-Evaluation Counseling[2] and had just started the required therapy of processing the events of my childhood. The work-shop leader picked me out to work in front of the group when she noticed that I'd started to cry during another woman's story about the death of her husband. She asked me if this woman's situation reminded me of anything.

The first thing that happened as soon as she started to work with me was that the tears stopped, and I didn't feel a thing. Why should I...this wasn't about me! She asked again. "Did you ever lose someone close to you? Think, think. Blank. Think again. "The only person I can think of is.........my grandfather!"

As I said those two words, a wave of grief rose up and out of me that couldn't be stopped. I went into a flood of crying that seemed bottomless, and even when the class was over I kept crying through lunch and for the rest of the day at the workshop.

Prior to this, I'd had no idea that the death of my grandfather had meant so much to me as a child. I was

2  Re-evaluation Counseling is a form of peer counseling where individuals are trained to exchange time and focused attention in order to assist each other to become free from emotionally painful past experiences. The system also includes group dynamics skills and awareness of social justice movements.

to work on this subject in my counseling sessions time and time again, discovering layer after layer of areas where it had affected me. I discovered that when he died he took my safety with him, leaving me feeling frightened and abandoned. As a little girl, I had not understood why he never said goodbye. To me it seemed as though he'd just disappeared without saying a word. How could he do that if he loved me?

And I missed him, oh, how that little girl missed him.

# A Concentration Camp for Cats

The absolute best friend of my childhood was my cat, Nosy. I think she got her name just because she had a little gray spot on her nose. Both of my parents worked, and this meant that I would often have some time alone at home after school until my mother and brother came home, and then lastly my father. Greeting me after I was let off the school bus by our country home was my cat.

She never ceased to fascinate me. She was very good at having kittens. I would follow this process very attentively, preparing different places for her to give birth. But usually she would always find some other more hidden place that she felt safer with and then I would have to go hunting for her to see how far along she was.

I remember one time she let me stay with her. I could see that she was in pain...I could see it in her eyes. As soon as the kittens came out she started licking them and then they somehow found their way to her nipples so she could start feeding them. This was all going on down in our basement cellar, and I would intermittently run up the stairs to report to my mother and brother about the latest events. I don't think they were all that interested.

In reminiscing about my cat as an adult, I would often say that it was my cat who taught me how to be a mother. My own mother never breast fed me (it was not "in vogue" at the time) and we had a lot of power struggles. But when I watched my cat with her kittens, there was only one thing I

Here I am with my beloved cat, "Nosy". She was rather homely and skinny, but I loved her with all my heart. I must be about six or seven years old in this photo.

40

could see, and that was love…unconditional love. She watched over them nervously and cleaned them and fed them. So then I had not only my cat to play with, but even her kittens.

One of my games was to try to get the kittens to go to sleep. I took it as a challenge…getting the kitten to fall asleep even though it had just been awake a moment ago. I would lay the kitten on its back and then stroke its tummy until it fell asleep. (This could very well have been my training as a healer since I would later in life lay my hands on people to help them with health problems. After this treatment, my clients will often say that they sleep very well the following night.)

We would find homes for the kittens, and this system worked out well, up to a certain point. One day my mother started saying that they would have to take Nosy away. She had too many kittens, and it was too difficult to find homes for them. Even though I was a child, I found out from someone that a cat could have an operation so it wouldn't have any more kittens. I remember standing beside my mother as she was preparing food in the kitchen, pleading with her…couldn't we get the cat an operation? The answer was no. I could tell from my mother's determination that there was no point in asking again.

We rode somewhere in our Ford from some forgotten year of the 1950s. My father was driving. My mother was in the front passenger seat. I was in the back seat with my cat Nosy and her last kitten in a box. The car stopped, and my father got out to open the back door. I pushed the lock down so that he couldn't take my cat and her kitten. He yelled at me to unlock the door. I didn't. He then walked around to the other side of the car, opened that door and took out the box. It all happened so fast, and I was powerless to do anything about it. My mother remained in front in silence, looking straight ahead. I watched as my cat was taken into a building that I somehow knew was for unwanted cats and kittens. That was the last time I saw her.

During my counseling sessions, I could feel that the murder of my best friend was right up there on a pain level with my grandfather dying. For years, I blamed my father since he was the one who actually removed the cats from the car. But as I continued to study the relationship between my mother, father and myself, I realized that it was in fact my mother who was the driving force behind the whole thing. The deeper mechanics of our relationship most likely played a part, but as an adult, I can now see her role as a working mother, an excellent housekeeper, and a loyal wife to her husband who was putting in extra work hours writing his doctoral thesis. She just didn't want to have to deal with finding homes for a mess of kittens, and perhaps my father had said that they could not afford an operation. But as a child, the loss of my best friend was very, very difficult. How could they take her away? How could they? Once again, I couldn't understand. Once again, I felt abandoned.

# Jesus Loved Children

In a way, our home was one of religious tolerance, since my mother, whose roots were Finnish, was Protestant and my French Canadian father was Catholic. But when my parents married, my mother had to sign papers promising that she would allow her children to be raised Catholic. So every Sunday my brother and I would have to get dressed up and packed off to Sunday Mass with our father. Mother stayed home, not being a regular church goer.

Growing up under the influence of the Catholic Church was, for me, a mixed world of horror and loving light. I remember having to kneel during prayers for long periods of time with bare knees on hard wooden benches that were covered with small stones from other people's shoes.

And then there were the sermons. One particular sermon is deeply etched in my memory bank: the priest, Father Dyer, was doing us the favor of trying to describe what it would be like to be in Hell. I was probably about five or six years old at the time. He said that we should light a match, and try to hold our finger in the burning flame. And then he said that Hell was like that, except a thousand times hotter, and if we died with mortal sins on our souls, we would have to stay there forever.

After Mass, I had to attend Catechism class in church. Here the children were gathered together to be instructed in Catholicism without the interference of any parents. I can still see the Catechism book in my lap. There was a picture of a boy, his heart illustrated with little black spots in it. The small black spots were called venial sins, which were small sins. On the next page, there was a picture of a little boy whose heart was completely black. This child's heart was black because he had committed a mortal sin; a very serious and big sin it was explained to us. The teacher, whom I am sure, meant well, wanted to protect us small children by making it clear that if we did not go and confess our sins to the priest and say our prayers of penance then we would, in fact, go to Hell and burn there forever when we died. (And just in case Catholics had any confusion surrounding what was a venial sin or a mortal sin, a long list was provided for handy guidance.)

Easter Sunday, and Mom has dressed me up to go to church. After Mass was celebrated, all the little kids were gathered for "Catechism class" where we were duly indoctrinated about the perils of dying with sins on our souls.

When I was 16, my Catholic girlfriends and I still had to go to Catechism classes. We had started kissing our boyfriends and according to the church if that activity became too passionate, well, it was a mortal sin. We also tried cigarettes, and that, too, was a sin of course. I remember my girlfriend asking the priest, "What do you think engaged couples do, Father? Hold hands?" His reply was, "That's why the church does not encourage long engagements." I had enough and started to consider leaving the church. Amazingly, young people in the United States are allowed to get their driving licenses at 16, so once that was achieved

I borrowed the family car and drove off to a larger city to go to confession somewhere where the priest wouldn't recognize my voice behind the dark curtain of the confessional.

I told this priest that I could not accept what the church was teaching about sinning and that I felt each person had to figure out for themselves what was right and what was wrong and try to follow that code.

The priest was furious with me.

"Do you mean to tell me that you can just go out and kill someone and that that's OK if you don't think it is a sin?" he said angrily. "I didn't say that," I said. I didn't have another answer to his challenge, but knew how far I'd gotten with my own analysis, and just repeated what I'd said earlier: "I think everyone needs to try to decide what is right and wrong for themselves, and try to follow that." He gave me a whole rosary (many prayers) to say as penance and dismissed me by saying "God Bless You!" in a tone of disgust.

I went out into the benches of the church which were empty at the time, and said all of the prayers, but from that moment on, in my heart I was no longer a member of the Catholic Church. Many years later, my father also left. Up to that time he had attended Sunday Mass regularly, but that changed after working decades as a psychologist. He had tested many children with Down's Syndrome which is a genetic disorder more common in children with older mothers. And yet, the official stance of the Catholic church was that the use of any form of contraception is a mortal sin. Over and again my father had tested Down's children whose aging Catholic parents had felt forced to choose between creating larger and larger families or burning in Hell forever. He finally got fed up with this policy and also stopped going to church.

After rehashing all of this in my therapy sessions, I checked to see if there was anything at all positive about being raised Catholic. I would have to say yes, there was. Beyond all of the descriptions of Hell, the Sunday school teachers also told us that Jesus was the son of God and that he loved children. Jesus was someone I could feel safe with as a child. Being the son of God was the same as being God, I thought. As I grew into my early teens, I still hated having to go to the confessional, but loved the ritual of going to communion. Taking the bread symbolic of Christ's body into my mouth, I could feel God's forgiveness and unconditional love.

Still, even though I don't like to spend much time mulling over what parts of my life I regret or dislike, I do wish that I had not been raised Catholic. I am sure that a love of God and some form of spiritual training could have been developed without the heavy conditioning involving so much guilt. What real good can come of giving small children so much fear?

# A Young Woman in a Child's Body

My teen years were stormy, and they started before I became a teenager chronologically. I was maturing quickly and already had developing breasts at the age of nine. This frightened my parents into laying down all sorts of rules that were designed to hold back the impossible, which was that my growth into a young woman started about four years earlier than they thought it should have. My father and I had always had a warm, close relationship, and each day used to start with a big hug. But around this time he stopped hugging me. I never found out why. One guess is that he might have become aroused and was frightened of his own reaction. Another possibility was that his classical training as a psychologist influenced him. At any rate, I now feel that it was a great mistake. I never felt anything inappropriate in relation to my father's way of expressing his love for me as a daughter and always felt completely safe with him. But I think the removal of his physical affection meant that I started seeking it elsewhere. I became very interested in boys and wanted to wear make-up already at the age of thirteen.

My mother tried to control me more and more and the more she tried to control me the more rebellious I became. Our relationship was tense and angry most of the time. A common pattern was that I would be verbally impertinent and she would hiss at me, "Don't you talk that way to your mother!" Once she hit me over the head with the blunt end of a knife at the dinner table. I can't remember what I'd said that time. On Memorial Day when I was only thirteen, I opened a bottle of allergy pills and took lots of them. I didn't come anywhere near dying, but got pretty messed up bio-chemically. I cried and cried, and my parents were shocked that I would try anything like that.

They refused to change any of their holiday plans and dragged me around with them to the Memorial Day parade and various other traditional events, saying simply to their friends that I wasn't feeling well. That was a very rough day. I remember Mom sitting by the side of my bed in the evening, talking with me. She was gentler and more understanding than usual…it seems as though I had felt driven to something quite drastic in order to bring down the level of tension between us.

Unfortunately, I never felt safe with my mother during the stormy, teenage years. Later on in life, after working through a lot of my difficulties with her as I trained to become a therapist, I was able to forgive and love her, which vastly improved our relationship. But during the "formative" years, I couldn't feel that she understood me, or was an ally. When I moved away from home to attend university, I was finally able to be on my own without my parents' constant interference. The first two years of college I lived in somewhat protected situations, but during the third year I got an apartment of my own and was in seventh heaven. I painted and decorated, sanded the floors, and my paternal grandmother made beautiful curtains. (Thank you Grammy!)

Water skiing at Branch Lake, Maine, where we had our summer cottage. I'm 15 years old.

During the hours and hours of telling and re-telling my life story with my co-counselors, a repetitive pattern began to emerge. I could see that the people whom I had trusted and who had provided safety in my life were generally men. Those who had treated me unkindly were women, the first experience of which was my mother's choice not to breastfeed me. My mother was responsible for killing my cat. My mother used to hit me. My grandmother wanted to hit me. Early in the morning, when I was a little girl and crawled into my parents' bed, it was my father I cuddled up to, not my mother. Who protected me from getting "the belt"? My grandfather. At night time, when I was scared and called out to my parents who slept across the hall, it was my father who came to comfort me. In short, whenever I was frightened and needed support, it had been a man who had provided the safety. Even God had a male identity, in the form of Jesus Christ, His only son.

# The First Contact

The first time a guru entered my world was through an ad in a Boston newspaper. I was in my third year at university. "Lecture on Transcendental Meditation as taught by Maharishi Mahesh Yogi," it said, and there was a small picture of a bearded man. I got out my dictionary to look up "transcendental."

"To go beyond," it said. Then I looked up Yogi. That came from Yoga, which meant "union." Immediately I felt attracted to these words and decided to go to the lecture. A neatly dressed, articulate man by the name of Jerry Jarvis held the lecture and spoke about being able to experience *the source of thought* through this meditation.

He also mentioned that meditating would make it easier to concentrate on studies and a number of other benefits that I didn't really pay much attention to. It was the expression "experiencing the source of thought" that drew my attention, and I decided without hesitation to take the course.

I waited until the summer of 1968 to actually enroll…having somehow known that I would need some extra space in my life to start the technique in the right way. I remember getting myself to someone's apartment somewhere in Cambridge, Massachusetts to take my first lesson. I also remember what my teacher looked like although I have forgotten his name. He had a neat haircut and a dark maroon jacket on. It was a warm summer day. The window was open, and I could hear children playing outside. The heavy, sweet smell of Indian incense filled the room.

With me were the flowers, fruit and white handkerchief the organization requested we bring since a ceremony would be performed on the first day. Standing beside my teacher, I watched with interest as he moved rice, incense, and a lit candle around, presenting these things as well as what I had brought, to the picture of an old man sitting with his legs in a crossed position. He repeated words in another language that I did not understand. Once the ceremony, or puja as it is called in India, was completed I sat down and waited for my teacher to say something. I had decided in advance that I would in no way try to convince myself of any effects with regard to the technique. I would simply follow this man's instructions and see what happened. He

then gave me a mantra, or a word, and told me how to use it. After a few minutes of practice, I was sent off alone to sit and meditate by myself.

I was very fortunate. From my very first meditation, I had a deep experience of "coming home." Sinking like a stone, I arrived spontaneously in a space that was unending, silent, peaceful, and loving, all at the same time. And the great thing was that that was inside of me! There was no fear!

The teacher's assistant came and got me after about 20 minutes...and I was upset that they had disturbed me. I just wanted to stay there and keep meditating; it was so delicious.

# A Change
# in Direction

After a few months of regular meditation and without giving it much thought, I one day realized that I had become much more creative, confident and empathetic as a person. A morbid fear of death that had been with me since childhood had also just dissipated, which was a tremendous relief. Even though I had been raised with the idea that personal development was something to be valued and encouraged, I had no idea that human consciousness could change so quickly and on such deep levels.

Many of my classmates at university were seeking expansion of consciousness by experimenting with different drugs, the most popular of the times being marijuana and LSD. I tried marijuana but fortunately found it unpleasant. We had been told by our TM teachers that meditation and drugs did not go well together, and my short trials seemed to verify that idea. So instead of going to parties to drop acid, I started attending meetings at the Cambridge meditation center. We would meditate together as a group and then share a meal. I discovered that vegetarian food can be very tasty and learned to drink herbal teas. The center leaders told us that it was possible to travel to India and become a teacher of meditation. As soon as I heard this, I knew that that was what I wanted to do. Originally, my career plan after getting my degree in Design had been to work with emotionally disturbed children as I had done during summer vacations. But in terms of personal development, meditation seemed to work so much faster!

So I applied for the Teacher Training Course and completed my senior year as I waited for the results of my application.

I remember graduating from college as one of the happiest days of my life. Finally, I could start living a life of my own, which hopefully would soon include an international trip to a faraway land. My father was appalled when he heard of my plans. To this day I can still see clearly his reaction as he sat across from me at the dinner table in my apartment in Boston. Angrily he said, "If you think I am going to give you one penny toward that trip…"

I interrupted him quickly and said, "I hadn't planned on asking you for money. I'm going to work and make the money myself." I must have anticipated his reaction since my decision to earn the money for the trip myself was already made. End of discussion.

My parents were quite nice people really, my father a psychologist and my mother a special education teacher. They had both grown up during the Great Depression and had their feet firmly attached to the ground. Particularly my father was very concerned with making our family's world financially safe and secure. Still, I never felt that my family understood me, or that I could talk to them about the thoughts and feelings that were moving through my mind. I felt wrong and out of place. I'd often escape to my room with books about fantasy and magic, reading alone for hours and hours on end. When I was ten years old, I wrote a story about a multi-colored flying horse that ended with the necessity of the horse flying back to the gods amidst thunder and lightning as I remained on the ground, tears streaming down my face saying good bye, good bye. I guess you could say that my head was already in the clouds.

# Anxious Waiting

My application for the Teacher Training Course was followed by a long period of waiting. I assumed that there was some sort of screening process upheld by SIMS (the Students' International Meditation Society based in California) and was very much afraid that, for some reason, I would not be accepted to become a teacher of meditation. As the months passed, I heard of a medium that could see into the future and decided to ask her what she saw for me.

This was my first experience of going to a medium, and the possibility of something magical happening was exciting. When I entered the appointment room, I was greeted by an elderly lady who seemed to have bad eyesight…it was as though her eyelids almost covered her eyes. She wore thick glasses and had difficulty walking. But she was such a sweet person. I remember feeling the gentleness and humility in her soul. She started by describing some of the objects in my apartment, most likely to establish that she did have psychic ability. One of the objects she described was a large multi-colored abalone shell which I did indeed have in my home. From that point on, I was convinced and listened attentively to what she had to say.

She spoke of seeing an open umbrella being shut and said that that meant the removal of protection. She followed this by saying that she saw me gathering flowers, spiritual bouquets she called them. "I see you making many, many spiritual bouquets," she said. I didn't understand much of what she was talking about, but asked at the end if she could see whether or not I had been accepted into the teachers' training program. Yes, she thought that I would be accepted. It wasn't a promise, but it was enough to keep me calm. Thanking her, I felt relieved and encouraged as I left.

# A Door Opens

*"Dear Judy,*

*Your application has been accepted for the course in India which begins January 7 and will be completed April 7, 1970. If your plans should change and you are unable to attend this course, please let us know as soon as possible..."*

My excitement knew no bounds. Now I just had to somehow get the course fee together quickly enough to join the training. The remaining time frame to find the money was only two months! In anticipation of being accepted, I had found work during the fall as a waitress in the cocktail lounge at the Boston Sheraton Hotel since I had heard that cocktail waitresses got generous tips from their customers.

That job was truly a test of how much I wanted to make the trip to India and become a teacher of meditation.

The environment in the lounge was very posh and exclusive, but to my horror I had to wear a special costume. Even though I was young and attractive, I felt very embarrassed about having to run around in an outfit that was supposed to make the waitresses look like Persian dancers. One of the girls even wanted me to put a big, white rhinestone in my navel, but no, that was going too far.

I felt different from the people working there. The customers were generally kind and appreciative, but my co-workers gave me a hard time about my plans to go to India to become a teacher of meditation, and some of them were downright nasty. A customer who came up to the bar one night asked what my favorite drink was. The bartender overheard this and replied before I had a chance to say anything, "Putz!" (And if you don't know what that means you can look it up in the urban dictionary. I don't even want to define it anymore.)

Another evening an elderly couple was taking some time to decide on what they wanted to order, and I was politely answering their questions about the different drinks. Simultaneously, there was a rather rowdy group of four people at a table in my area that wanted another round of drinks, NOW. They complained to

# SIMS
### Students' International Meditation Society

National Headquarters • 1015 Gayley Avenue • Los Angeles, California 90024 • 478-1569

November 5, 1969

Dear Judy:

Your application has been accepted for the course in India which begins January 7 and will be completed April 7, 1970. If you plans should change and you are unable to attend this course, please let us know as soon as possible.

The course fee is $550.00 (U.S.) which will be due before December 7, 1969. The procedure for paying the course fee is as follows: a bank draft, certified check or cashier's check should be made payable to SRM Foundation of India and sent directly by registered air mail to

> American Express International Banking Corp.
> SRM Foundation of India Account
> Connaught Place
> New Delhi, India

Immediate notification of your payment should be made to Terry Gustafson, SIMS - Los Angeles.

Course participants are expected to arrive in New Delhi by January 7 and rest that night at the Ranjit Hotel, Maharajah Ranjit Singh Road, New Delhi (phone 277981), where accommodations will be reserved. The party will leave for the Academy by deluxe buses on January 8 at 9 a.m., arriving around 5 p.m.

The course will continue at the Academy until it is completed on April 7. Those desiring to visit Kashmir or other parts of India following the course will be expected to make their own arrangements.

A complete itinerary of an around-the-world tour that has been worked out in cooperation with Maharishi will be sent to you soon. The tour provides an excellent opportunity for a smoother, more economical and interesting way to travel to India via the world. Participants may leave from any point in the United States or Canada and assemble as a group in San Francisco or Hawaii for departure for stays in Tokyo and Hong Kong and then on to New Delhi. Following the course, the tour will continue to Srinagar, Kashmir, Agra, Jaipur, Bombay and then on through the Middle East and Europe.

As soon as you receive the tour information, please carefully study this opportunity and contact Giselle's Travel in Sacramento or Air-India in San Francisco for any additional help and information. These two agencies are familiar with the travel of course

... at the Academy will be vegetarian. Those desiring any food supplements or special types of foods should bring their own.

For any additional information concerning the course, contact SIMS,

<u>and</u>

Jai Guru Dev

Jerry Jarvis
Director

the hostess of the room that they had to wait too long. This hostess, my boss, was perfectly coiffed and perfectly dressed. She immediately took me behind the scenes and said, "If you want to keep this job you'd better get the lead out of your ass!"

One night I finally broke down in tears and called my parents. My father listened patiently, but he didn't promise to assist financially. Shortly afterwards I quit because I just couldn't stand it any longer, and was still a little short of the necessary funding. My dad must have taken pity on me in the end since he agreed to purchase my high-end stereo set with fantastic speakers that I had bought two years earlier with my own money, and that rounded off the final sum that I needed to make the trip to India. I had already sold or given away most of my belongings since I felt that I would not be returning home for a very long time. (That certainly turned out to be true.)

My poor parents...they drove me to the airport to see me off, their "little girl" who had never traveled outside of the United States. It was the first time I would fly in an airplane! I'd be traveling alone for a month in Europe until I connected with the teachers' group in India. Their faces looked ashen gray as they stood in front of me to say goodbye. Now, as I parent, I certainly understand why. They were right of course. Anything could happen to a 22-year-old American girl traveling alone on her first trip to Europe and India.

# In India for the First Time

Everything in India was so different from my North American background. In my country people used porcelain dishes, knives and forks when they ate food. During my first meal in India, we sat on the floor, eating our food off a huge banana tree leaf with our bare hands (or hand I should say...the right hand was used with the left remaining passive in one's lap since that was the hand you were supposed to use for washing your bottom). At home, it was fine for a woman to wear a short skirt and show her legs. In India women had to cover their bodies and wear sarees, a traditional, draped cloth dress.

The air smelled smokey whenever we were near a

village. I found out that was burned, dried cow dung used as fuel. And the food was different, hot and spicy. Even the toilets were different. Western toilets were like comfortable chairs; an Indian toilet was a hole in the floor! Hey, where's the toilet paper? I was in another world, a world where my everyday life would quickly alternate between curious excitement and...yuuck!

Once at the Ashram I tried to make my small, simple room cozy. It was cold at night since we were in north-

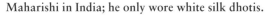
Maharishi in India; he only wore white silk dhotis.

ern India and it was January. From my window, I heard some weird howling off in the distance that sounded like ghosts or witches. It scared the living daylights out of me. The next day I asked someone what that sound was I'd heard during the night and was told that it was "just" hyenas.

I remember one of the German girls showing me how to use a hot water bottle to put in the bed. I had never seen a hot water bottle before in my life. She demonstrated carefully how to fill it and press the hot water up to the brim so as not to have too much air in it. She was surprised at my ignorance about such matters. "You Americans!" she said with disdain. I was very thankful to learn about this new contraption since, in January, the bed was wretchedly cold and damp at night.

Shortly after our arrival we were told that Maharishi wanted us all to come to his home where we were to meet him for the first time. I was so excited! Having been raised Catholic, I thought I was going to meet a modern, living ecquivalent of Jesus Christ. We were instructed to get ourselves down to his house, which was located at the bottom of a gentle slope, at some distance from the rooms where we were staying. We had all been waiting for some time, packed into Maharishi's spacious living room, sitting on the floor. He suddenly swept through the door saying "Jai Guru Dev!". This greeting was used by everyone in the TM movement. It means simply, "Hail Guru Dev." Guru Dev was the short name for Maharishi's own guru, Swami Brahmananda Saraswati, Jagadguru Bhagwan

Shankaracharya of Jyotir Math, to whom he always gave credit when speaking about the Transcendental Meditation technique.

Maharishi exuded joy and energy as he stood there in front of us, dressed in his white silk dhotis[3], and explained that we would come out to meet with him a few minutes, one by one.

I was sitting by the door. As he turned and started walking out through the door, he looked right at me and said softly, "Come!" I asked the woman sitting beside me, one of the coordinators for the Cambridge area, if she thought he meant me. She said," No, I don't think so." So I sat and waited my due turn to go out into the garden for the individual appointment. Maharishi was sitting there behind a small table he used as a desk, and I sat down nervously in the empty chair.

"What took you so long?" he asked.

"Well, I had to wait my turn." I said.

"I was *waiting…*" he said with his famous giggle.

I didn't know what to say. I could hardly breathe. He asked about my education and background and seemed to be very pleased with whatever I said…beyond that I can no longer remember what we talked about. As I walked back to my room, my stomach was churning with mixed feelings of surprise and joy. Maharishi seemed to like me!

---

3  Traditional Indian dress for men comprised of a 4-5m long sarong, usually white or cream colored. It can be worn in several draping styles. Maharishi always wore white silk dhotis.

# Down in the Cave

After the first meeting in the garden, what was happening between us started to move along very quickly. Maharishi sent a messenger to let me know that I could see him for a private consultation. When I arrived at his villa, he greeted me and led me through his home to a room in the cellar that was called his "cave". We walked over the large oriental carpet past a guard sitting on the floor of the living room who appeared to be dead asleep. I remember thinking about that afterward. It was so strange that this man did not hear us walking within inches of his face. Normally everyone was "on their toes" so to speak around Maharishi, always ready, willing and able to serve. But not this guard, and not now. He was out cold. We went down some stairs to a small room in the basement with no windows. The energy felt very good there in spite of the room being rather dark. My memory is that there was a small altar there with a picture of Guru Dev and some candles were lit next to his picture.

On the way in I knocked over a glass of Maharishi's water that was on the floor and felt wretchedly embar-

**Maharishi's villa.**

rassed. Beyond trying to recover from feeling so clumsy, I just waited to see what was going to happen next.

It was my impression that he was going to give me some kind of advanced meditation technique. By this time, I had definitely noticed that I was getting special attention but still didn't understand why.

Maharishi had me sit on the floor to his left, and started by asking how everything was going with my meditation...our dialogue was undramatic. Suddenly he raised his hand and began stroking my hair, which was then very long. I felt myself flush. It was at that point that I finally realized the reason I was getting special attention might have something to do with me being a woman and him being a man. He laughed a little and was obviously a bit nervous. "Don't tell anyone," he said, and I agreed. "No, I won't tell anyone."

# The New Favorite

Overnight I had become the new favorite. I wasn't aware then of Maharishi's habit of gathering people around him that he was fond of for different reasons. (Nor did I know that one's allotted moment of being given permission to shine in the Master's presence could at any time just go "Poof"!) Favorites were members of the inner circle. When their physical presence was desired they were called, and they came.

One such person was Jerry Jarvis, the leader of the Students' International Meditation society, with its headquarters based in Los Angeles, California. It was through Jerry that I had first started to meditate.

Another was Jemima Pitman, a wealthy English woman of exceptional upbringing and character. Jemima was a very special woman in the life of Maharishi Mahesh Yogi. I sincerely doubt that they ever had a romantic relationship, and yet they were very close. According to Ashram gossip, she was the only one who could get Maharishi to take silence (rest and meditate). It was as though she was Maharishi's "white marriage" wife and mother, all rolled into one. He called her "Ma."

Jerry was with us now in India; Jemima I had only heard about. There was another English woman whom Maharishi always called upon when he wanted to dictate a book or some other text to be published. Her name was Carol, and she was also with us now in India. Then there were the various "Skin Boys," young men whose responsibility it was to follow Maharishi's movements from one place to another in order to be able to quickly throw down a patch of fur for his Holiness to sit on. Skin Boys would also fill the role of quickly meeting whatever practical needs that might have spontaneously arisen. It was all so new for me, Maharishi's world.

I remember a sweet German girl, Helene, as one of the first to show a reaction to Maharishi's interest in me. She had attended the Teacher Training Course before this one and was back for more. When she spoke to me, it was as though she was thinking aloud, without censoring her thoughts.

"I have to be friends with you. Maharishi likes you, and so if I want still to be here with him, I must be

Above: A trader is showing his wares to Maharishi and the inner circle in India, 1968 or 69. Jemima is to his right in the picture.

Left: Jerry Jarvis is in the upper right of the picture.

friends with you." I could sense her anxiety, but didn't give it much consideration. I was so filled with the pleasant feelings of having all of my neurotic needs for love and attention being more than adequately met at the time.

We never did become close friends in spite of her good intentions. I think she stopped trying to be near Maharishi and just sort of allowed herself to fade into the background. This teacher training course must have been a painful three months for her due to Maharishi making such a fuss over me. I have since tried to find out what became of her, but no one seems to know.

# Courtship

Some of us got to go along on a trip to New Delhi with Maharishi. We were going to visit an Indian family who were devotees. This must have been in January 1970 since I was still dressed in the only saree I had purchased up to that point. It was made of the simplest, most inexpensive cotton, which was all that could be afforded on a tight budget. In those days the course fee was not exorbitant but still, I was fresh out of college and had just managed to scrape together enough money to get to India.

The home we were visiting was quite luxurious and comfortable. Their house was spacious, and they had a Western style toilet! We were treated with great

# HOW TO WEAR A SAREE

**SAGA DEPARTMENT STORES LTD.**
251, T.T.K. Road, Alwarpet,
Chennai - 600 018. India
Tel : 91-44-499 3811, 4971389/90
Fax : 91-44-4971387

## 1

The world's most graceful dress for women is just six yards of untailored cloth. A few deft operations and you step forth with poise and presence. Here in these pages is the secret of how to do it.

## 2

### A CLOCKWISE TURN

Holding the saree (which is going towards the left) close to your waist turn full circle towards the right in a clockwise direction; thus winding it once around the body and just overlapping the inner edge. Tuck in into the petticoat, carefully maintaining an even level at the bottom in front as well as at the back. While not losing any neatness, the saree should not be pulled too tightly around the hips. To ensure this small pleat can be made at the back and tucked in neatly.

### MAKE KNIFE PLEATS

Now make seven to ten knife pleats, each pleat being approximately five inches wide But before you start pleating, be careful to mark off a length of two yards or less from the pallau end for pasing across the shoulder.

## 3

This is one of the few ways of pleating:

(a) Hold the top edge of the saree going towards the left, between the forefinger and the middle finger of the right hand which are stretched out in front while the thumb goes back to join the little finger and the third finger. Fold it over the forefinger and pass it under and around the thumb.

(b) Now bring it back to the front and remove the forefinger from its former position to place it over the top edge again, so that the first fold and the beginning of the second should be between the middle finger and the forefinger.

(c) Repeat this six to eight times to make seven to ten pleats leaving about two yards of the saree free to pass round the hips and across the shoulders.

## 4

### TUCK THEM IN

Gather the pleats evenly and neatly and tuck them into the petticoat slightly towards the lefts side but not too much on the left side. See that the breadth of the pleats is equal and that they are piled on top of each other evenly. The lower edge of the pleats should also be even and just off the ground. The Gracefulness of the saree depends mainly on these pleats and the way they are made.

### ANOTHER TURN

Having tucked in the pleats, turn around again to the right holding the top edge of the saree in your hand and bring it round your hips to the front.

### OVER THE SHOULDER

Gather the Pallau and place it over the left shoulder letting it fall gracefully behind and

## 5

over the left arm covering most of it. The upper border of the saree shouls slant across the bust from under the right arm to over the left shoulder. The pallau should be about a yard in length, just touching the finger-tips, if it falls evenly behind.

### AND NOW IN FULL BEAUTY

The saree, when correctly worn, the Pallau can also be gathered and flung over the shoulder where it can be held in place with a pin or it can be brought round the right shoulder to the front revealing its full beauty.

77

reverence...these people were obviously thrilled to have Maharishi visiting them.

But Maharishi was not pleased with my attire. He said to the women in this family, "Show her how to wear a saree." There was a slight note of disdain in his voice, read "Good God, look at the way she's dressed!"

Apparently he expected me to learn the customs of this land. I followed the women into one of the family bedrooms to receive instruction. Dressing oneself in this traditional feminine attire was no simple matter, at least not for someone from the West. Our hostesses showed me patiently how to wrap the cloth and then

Here I am still wearing an inexpensive, purple cotton sari. Maharishi hasn't started dressing me up yet, so this must be at the very beginning of our three-month Teacher Training Course in Rishikesh.

make pleats with my hand, then to tuck it into my slip so that it would be the right length.

The following days were filled with much practicing. It took quite a while before I could get up some speed in wrapping myself in the yards of folded cloth, or feel comfortable walking around in this outfit. I finally devised a system of pinning the saree here and there so as to be able to relax and not have think about whether or not the blasted thing would stay hanging right. That was step one.

Another day Maharishi started to complain that the cloth in my saree was too course...it should be silk.

Various traders and tailors would come to the Ashram quite regularly to sell their goods to the Westerners, so I purchased a pink saree of silk.

Once purchased and displayed, Maharishi said that the silk should be of better quality. Soon thereafter he introduced me to an Indian couple whom he said

This was my very first silk saree purchased at the ashram. He didn't think the quality of the silk was good enough and sent me to Delhi with money to get something better.

would take me to town and assist me to purchase some silk sarees and gold jewelry. I can't remember whether he gave me the money directly or whether he gave it to my hosts, but at any rate there was no talk of having a limit as to how much to spend.

We spent the whole day in New Delhi. This family took me to reputable traders who showed me silk of high quality. I tried to select colors that looked rather celestial, thinking Maharishi would surely be pleased, and ordered some simple gold bracelets.

Back at the Ashram I dressed in my new attire. Alone again with him, I expected that he would approve. Yes, yes...this was good, but the silk should be "tinner". And the bracelets were too thick. I should have a thin, gold necklace, and the bracelets should be more delicate.

Another trip to New Delhi. I went back to the goldsmith and asked if he could make the bracelets thinner, and commissioned a gold chain necklace with some coral beads. At the saree shop, I discovered transparent silk chiffon and bought one in bright pink, printed with small flowers.

Would Maharishi, on my fourth attempt to dress as he liked, be pleased?

"This is beautiful, bee-uu-tiful!!!" he burst out. Finally! I was happy and relieved. Looking back at it now, it was as though he wanted me dressed as etherically as possible; everything should be of the best quality and most refined...goddess-like.

So suddenly I had gone from dressing like a poor, hippy artist to adorning myself with the finest Indian attire. Sometimes I wondered whether or not the other course members noticed the change. On the other hand, I didn't want to worry about what they thought. I only cared whether or not Maharishi was happy. Once the "right" style was established, he gave me money to buy silk chiffon sarees in a multitude of colors; white, lilac, deep purple with gold and red trim, as well as a red wedding saree with the most amazing sequined embroidery. I still have them, packed away in a special suitcase in the attic.

# Man and Woman

Just for the record, I never tried to seduce Maharishi. I think I loved him, or thought I loved him before I even met him, but not as a man, more as a divine human being. And when that "divine being" expressed attraction toward me as a woman, I started to fall in love with him as a man. For sure I have wondered what it was about my internal make up to have me react that way rather than feeling his behavior was inappropriate. Some years back I read a bit about my astrological chart and discovered that my Venus is in Pisces. There are lots of details attached to that, but one sentence, written by the astrologer John Townley, jumped out at me: "Your sexuality may become mixed with religious feelings."

This is how Maharishi wanted me dressed: silk chiffon and delicate gold bracelets.

I was certainly overwhelmed by my emotions, so much so that I wrote a love poem to him, garnished with spiritual terms. He loved it. Reading a poem for Maharishi became our excuse for time alone. At the end of his work day, if he had been dictating letters or some material for a new publication, he would suddenly say, "A poem, a poem!" and I knew that was my cue. Once alone, I would read what I had written for him, he would smile and laugh, and say "Come," patting the bed beside him.

The first time Maharishi and I were intimate is still a very private moment and I don't feel comfortable sharing the whole experience. Making the details a subject for anyone to gawk at brings it all down to an exhibitionistic level, which in my mind, removes the quality of love. Perhaps I was blind, but my experience was that we did indeed love each other. I am willing however to share enough to show that Maharishi, beyond being a world famous guru, was also just an ordinary man.

This time we met at night in his bedroom, not his meditation "cave." I don't remember anymore how I managed to get to his house without other people figuring out what was going on, but I remember what happened thereafter.

He struck me as not being an experienced lover... he just hugged me and kissed me with great enthusiasm and I could feel his desire. The first time we both kept our clothes on and engaged in a lot of petting of the type teenagers do in high school. I remember wondering how far this was going to go. In the wee hours

85

That's me walking beside Maharishi on the path at the Ashram
in Rishikesh, well hidden behind my master.

of the morning, our bodies finally joined as man and woman, and I felt both shocked and happy as I snuck back to my room. I felt so loved.

The next day I expected that all outer appearances would be as usual and got dressed for breakfast and then prepared to go to lectures. But the schedule of the day had been changed. Lectures were cancelled. Cancelled? Lectures had never been cancelled before…

I walked down to Maharishi's house and was let into his room. He was lying on his bed, surrounded by several Brahmacharis (male celibates) sitting on the floor. There could have been a total of five or six men around him. One was a hermit living in the surrounding mountains with hair so long it hung down in long, twisted ropes. Dressed only in a loin cloth, he was sitting on the floor by the end of the bed, massaging my guru's feet. The other Brahmacharis were dressed in white silk robes, just like Maharishi's. Maharishi looked tired and seemed to be ill, but after the night we had spent together, I didn't dare to say anything, certainly not in front of these men. I came back later when all of them had gone and asked him what was the matter…was he sick?

He responded, "Don't you see? The whole energy is used to going up!" and he swept his hand vertically, in front of himself. I didn't understand it then, but he was referring to the kundalini energy in his body, meaning that the life force usually traveled from his root chakra at the base of the spine up through his crown chakra at the top of the head. In other words, his sexual energy had moved down and out instead of up. He did not sound happy. And I felt terrible. What had we done? He stared off into nowhere for a moment with a distressed expression.

Then suddenly he seemed to let go of it, laughed a little and patted his bed again, wanting me to come close. We spent some time hugging, and I felt reassured that at least he did not suddenly hate me.

We continued to meet at night, but not every night. In the beginning he had someone come and get me, then later we usually managed to agree by exchanging a few words on the path. "You can come tonight?" he would say in a low voice.

After making love, I would stay for a couple of hours for small talk and a little sleep before sneaking back to my hut.

I remember at some point reflecting upon Maharishi's age as I was lying in his arms...he must have been around 52 and I was 22. "He's about the same age as my parents," I thought. But I didn't care. I was just so happy to be that close. I also thought about the fact that we came from two very different cultures. Once I asked him what the name was of the female genitals in Hindi.

"Yoni" he said. "And the male?" "Lingom". He was so embarrassed that I could hardly hear his whispered answer, even though no one else was there but us. It was very difficult for him to say these words out loud. He obviously knew what his own biology was called in English, but wanted to ask the name of my feminine. "Wagina," he repeated after me, like a young schoolboy.

# Complete Surrender

Some of you may wonder how I could fall so in love with this small man who was old enough to be my father? I have.

Maharishi was the first man that I allowed myself to love so completely once I had become a young adult. I think this was partly due to my mixing up the human Maharishi with my guru, Maharishi. Remember, Venus in Pisces. And I think I mixed him up with the other saviours of my childhood...first grandfather and then Jesus. And Jesus was in turn all blended in with a concept of God. Even though the God of my childhood was someone I had been forced to confess sins to, deep within I believed that no one listened to me as God

This was our lecture hall in Rishikesh. We listened to Maharishi's lectures here and shared meditation experiences. I felt more at home with many of the ideas from Hindu philosophy than I did with the ideas I had been raised with in the Catholic church.

did, no one could forgive me as God did, no one loved me as God did. God was safe.

If God was safe, Jesus was safe. If Jesus was safe, my guru was safe. If my guru Maharishi was safe, then Maharishi the man was safe; safe to receive love from and safe to love in return. Not that I was aware of any of this conditioning at the time, but something like that could have been running through the deeper portions of my psyche.

Maharishi would often lecture about the quality of love that a devotee should have for one's master. It was all about surrender, total and complete surrender. And, we, the listeners, could hear the devotion in his voice and see the love in his countenance when he spoke of this favorite subject. I think these talks were about the love he felt for his master, Brahmananda Saraswati, or Guru Dev as he was generally known to us. But as I listened I interpreted it to be about the kind of devotion I should have for my master. And when the man in him loved me as a woman that made it all even easier.

Listening and then reacting to those lectures was like slipping on a golden banana peel, as I allowed myself to fall more and more deeply in love.

I wrote more poems. I picked more flowers. I spent a lot of time picking anything that blossomed (if we were in an area where it was possible), and then threading each blossom through needle and thread to make garlands to place around Maharishis neck. Any excuse to express my feelings. I remember now how the elderly medium I had visited before leaving for India spoke of my making so many spiritual bouquets. She was right…that was how I spent a lot of my time.

Here we are, learning how to perform the puja ceremony at the ashram in Rishikesh. Filled with enthusiasm and devotion, we believed we would create peace in the world. I am waiting in the background.

© Jonathan Miller

# Strange Things Happening

One of the things that can easily happen when people meditate together on a Teachers' Training course is that they become quite clairvoyant in different ways. And we were meditating for hours on end as part of our preparation. I remember one woman describing how she suddenly saw herself in a past lifetime during her meditation…she was absolutely clear and convinced that that was what she had experienced. She said it was just like watching a movie. I was quite envious of her, since I believed in the theory of re-incarnation but had never had any experiences or memories of my own at that time.

From the group photo in Rishikesh. I'm sitting directly in front of Maharishi. I don't remember what the joke was.

One day a woman named Margo said that she had started to see through the walls of the Ashram. That made me nervous. In fact, once when I was waiting in line together with her to see Maharishi, as I went in before her she said to me with a big smile, "Give him a hug from me!" I was mortified. In shock, I just looked at her and didn't manage to get a word out. The next night we spent together I told Maharishi what she had said, and asked,

"What if she can see us together?"

"I don't think she will say anything," was his reply.

I tried to let go of worrying after that, but she definitely gave me the heebie jeebies. I found it remarkable that Maharishi could be so cool about the whole thing.

# Under the Stars

One night in particular sticks out amongst the memories. We had agreed that I would come to him once everyone was asleep. Looking back, I cannot understand how I managed this venture, being morbidly afraid of walking outside at night when alone. This fear is still with me, in spite of having worked through a lot of other insecurities. Maharishi's Ashram lay in the midst of a forest in the hills of Rishikesh, with Mother Ganges at a steep drop below us. At this point I knew that there were hyenas, tigers, spiders, scorpions and poisonous snakes around us, all of which course members had either seen or heard. In order to make the trek from my room over to Maharishi's house without being discovered, I had to leave my flip flop sandals behind. But walking barefoot was just too scary! So on went a pair of thick socks to provide some form of protection, in my mind at least. And then it was a question of which path to choose? There were several paths that led to his home. It was important to pick one where I wouldn't be seen.

My heart in my throat, I quietly tip-toed along the path, hoping that no one would notice me walking by. Although the actual distance was short, the fear made the walk seem like it was very long. I finally arrived at Maharishi's house in spite of the intense panic. He met me as I got there and led me up to the roof. The next thing I remember is being entwined in eachothers' arms and legs in a bed covered with mosquito net under the stars. I just lay there with him, divinely happy. He smelled so good. Not from any kind of applied scent such as after shave! HE smelled good. His skin, his breath, his hair. If there was any kind of smell that came from an outside influence, it could possibly have been Pear's soap.

Maharishi asked me a question. "Do you think I should become Prime Minister of India, or do you think I should remain a spiritual leader?" I could not believe what I had just heard. How could my Guru, Maharishi Mahesh Yogi, be asking *me* for advice? At any rate, I hid my reaction and just gave him my opinion. "I think you should remain a spiritual leader because that's what you're good at," I said. In later years, I would reflect on his question many, many times.

He seemed to be in the mood to talk. I mustered the

courage to ask him something that had been on my mind for several weeks. "Maharishi, what would you do if I became pregnant?" His answer was quick and ruthless. "Get married...quick." "To whom?" I asked. "Some good choice in the movement." That answer was the beginning of a wake-up call...just because Maharishi was smothering me with love and attention did not mean that we would ever have any kind of "normal" relationship, a message that was a disappointment for a young woman of child-bearing age. But I don't remember going into a spin over it...I probably had enough contact with reality to realize that most ordinary rules would not apply to this situation.

In this photo you can see the roof veranda of Maharishi's villa where we were together under the stars.

# A Few of Us Remained Longer in India

I didn't establish a lot of close friendships with the other course members during the 1970 Teachers' Training. The secret relationship with Maharishi isolated me emotionally, since I was very aware that it had to be kept secret. Most of my classmates probably viewed me as being rather aloof.

And then there was some kind of flurry well into the course, involving one of the Skin Boys, a young Indian man whom I will call Abhay.

Abhay loved Maharishi as we all did, and was very devoted in his role as Skin Boy. He lived in Maharishi's home, so in that sense you could say he was the Skin Boy who was closest to Maharishi at the time.

Graduating class 1970 International TM Teachers' Training course at Maharishi's Ashram in Rishikesh, India. Judith front row, to the right of MMY in photo. Rob McCutchen in the next to the last row, 2nd person to the right of the tree in photo.

99

Without warning or obvious cause, Abhay started to change his behavior. Earlier he was always very neat in his appearance, cleanly shaved with nicely pressed white shirts and black pants. Suddenly he stopped shaving regularly and looked very tired, like he had slept in the middle of a bus station somewhere. I noticed that he started reacting strangely toward me, and didn't understand why.

Perhaps I would have a note that I wanted to send to Maharishi or something similar, and he would abruptly turn around and start running in the other direction. At the time, it never occurred to me that he might know about what was going on between Maharishi and me, but recently ex-Skin Boy Rob gave me some explanation. The two young men had been close, the best of friends. Rob says he and Abhay had begun making jokes about me, calling me the "poetry girl." Then Abhay started saying he had lost faith in everything, in Maharishi and his movement, but Rob says he never said straight out that he had discovered Maharishi and I were sleeping together. I had noticed the change in Abhay but never really connected the dots.

And besides, who can think clearly when you are walking around in a golden bubble of bliss? There were really only two things that mattered to me at the time: first and foremost was my relationship with Maharishi. Secondly I was very committed to becoming a teacher of Transcendental Meditation. I took the training very seriously and listened carefully to what Maharishi said during the lectures, taking notes and completing all of the lessons that were required of us.

When the 3-month course was over, almost everyone traveled home to their countries of origin. A small number of us were however allowed to stay on an additional two months. We were about half women and half men. Several of the men decided to travel further in India to see famous places such as the Taj Mahal. I so wanted to go along to see the Taj, but Maharishi wouldn't allow it. He did not want the women traveling around on their own.

A trip to Bangalore in the south of India was scheduled. Maharishi would be giving a shorter course for Indian teachers of meditation. At that time, he was more well-known in the West than in India, and this course would be smaller and faster. It was also probably not as lucrative for him, since Westerners were always charged more for courses in India than the natives. It was just assumed that we all had more money than they did.

The last step of becoming a teacher of TM was receiving mantras personally from Maharishi, the mantras we were to use when we taught meditation. Those of us who remained behind after the larger group had left had our final initiation put off for a couple of weeks. We were just about to leave for Bangalore when my classmate Susan Seifert told Maharishi she did not want our final step to be put off until Bangalore and Maharishi replied, "You are right."

Thus it was that we were initiated as teachers on April 19, 1970, which was also my birthday. But more than any particular celebration of that event, what I remember most is the moment when Maharishi gave me my mantras. Once again we were sitting in one of the lower "cave" rooms, I on his left and he to my right. During this private session there was no funny business. Maharishi took it as seriously as I did and was very correct. I received the mantras, made sure that I knew how to pronounce them accurately, and set about committing them to memory. The passing on of Vedic Sanskrit mantras comes originally from an oral tradition, which is believed to have started thousands of years ago.

Shortly thereafter we all flew to Bangalore to accompany Maharishi on the Teacher Training course for Indians. This was the first time I would experience the scenario connected to whether or not one would get to go along on the next course with him. Anyone who was ever a member of the inner circle knows exactly what I am talking about. You either got to go along or you didn't and that decision rested with Maharishi and Maharishi alone. Until one knew who was going and who would be left behind or sent off to manifest some other movement related task, anxiety levels were high. I would often notice a lot of jealousy amongst members of the inner circle around Maharishi, and this way of handling us didn't make things better. At any rate, still riding high on my status as current favorite, I got to go along.

Bangalore was on the whole, a lovely experience. There were beautiful flowers on the trees everywhere in contrast to the rather arid feel of the Ashram in Rishikesh. Maharishi stayed at the homes of his devotees while the rest of us who were members of his entourage stayed at a nearby hotel. But we were still all invited to share some meals with these families at the same time as they had Maharishi as their guest. I found it difficult that the spices used in Southern India were much hotter, yet the dishes that were prepared for us were cooked with so much expertise and love! I don't think I have had such good cooking anywhere since during my six trips to India.

Our nights were spent at the hotel...one of which was rather luxurious in style, and tried to cater to Western tastes. This was a refreshing change from Maharishi's Ashram where everything was quite simple in those days. After three months of the vegetarian Ashram food I had started to fantasize like crazy about hamburgers, french fries, and ice cream. When I discovered that there was an Ice Cream Split on the menu at our hotel I got so excited! Vanilla, strawberry and chocolate ice cream, topped with bananas, chopped nuts, and chocolate sauce! Promptly thereafter ordered. Promptly thereafter consumed. Promptly thereafter puked up. Welcome to India.

There was very little opportunity for moments of intimacy during that trip. Maharishi and I had only one meeting alone during the two weeks we were there. Even I had to wait in line for a private audience during the day. When I finally sat with him, we just had a short conversation, but the verbal exchange was still rather intimate. When I left I discovered that an Indian man had been let in and was sitting on the floor, waiting behind a screen placed near us to speak with his guru. I was horrified...oh my God, he must have heard everything we said to each other!!! That event created a lot of nervousness for me during the following days, but I never heard any more about it. I think I managed to convince myself that this man could not speak English and therefore had not understood what Maharishi and I had said to each other. This balancing act of a secret life and an official life was nerve racking.

# Time
## to Leave India

Back at the Ashram in Rishikesh, the heat and then monsoon humidity increased during May. Our small group was now at the end of the 5th month of our stay with Maharishi. After returning from the Teachers' Training course in Bangalore, there was no set schedule, so the few of us that were there had more time to just hang out, with each other and with Maharishi. I remember lying on my bed under the mosquito net, looking at photos I had collected of Maharishi like a star struck teenager, dreaming about her latest idol. I would find excuses to write Maharishi small notes and have them sent off by messenger to his house.

Here is one that I saved:

*"Dearest Maharishi,*

*We received a note from you saying that we are confined to our rooms until 6.00 PM! Alright, but we shall miss you very much.*

*All love and Jai Guru Dev,*

*Judith & Nini (she was another member of the group who had stayed on past the 3-month Teachers' Training course)*

*P.S. Are you meditating?"*

His reply:

*"Sun is favourable—kinder—seeing you in the confinement of your room, if you like you can come out after 5 PM."*

These small notes worked in much the same way that lovers send each other text messages via cell phones today…if he wrote something back I would be happy for the rest of the day.

During these weeks I was a bit more social and friendly with the other girls who had also stayed on, all avid devotees. We moved to other quarters, a newer building with small apartments closer to Maharishi's house and actually had our own bathrooms! Susan

*Dearest Maharishi,*

*We received a note from you saying that we are confined to our rooms until 6:00 P.M.! Alright, but we shall miss you very much.*

*All love ; Jai Guru Dev*
*Judith ; Mimi*

*P.S. Are you meditating?*

*Sun is favourable – kinder – selling you in the confinement of your room, if you like you can come out afta.*

To His Holiness
Maharishi
Mahesh
Yogi

From Judith
& Mimi

I sent small notes via messengers to Maharishi, and he would return them with a reply. If he wrote something back I would be happy for the rest of the day! This one was dictated to Carole Hamby who wrote down his answer. They had been working on some manuscript when he got the note. It was so hot that he had told us not to come out of our rooms at the Ashram during the day.

Seifert was in a room near mine, so we ended up chatting a lot. She was fun to be with. Susan was deathly afraid of any kind of insect, and of course, who was the one who ran into most of the spiders and scorpions? Oddly, I never once saw a scorpion or big spider while I was there, and at the same time, the hot and humid air would be regularly punctuated with curdling screams coming from Susan's room when another unwelcome guest had made its entrance.

Susan Shumsky was also a part of this group. Susan was into astrology in those days, and I have one clear memory of a session with her where she had examined my horoscope. She looked down at her notes and said with a serious voice, "You need a strong, strong man." Little did she know (then) that I already had one.

Those were lazy, slow days. The heat prevented us from racing around, and the extreme temperature made me lose my appetite. The ice cream episode had left me with chronic digestive problems and in the end the only thing I wanted to eat was fresh mangoes. I ate so many mangoes that I got allergic to them and was soon covered with at least 5000 itchy red dots. I was growing weary of the food in India, the dirt in India, and now the oppressive climate that made me feel like I weighed a ton even though I was in fact ten kilos lighter. Walking from my room to the dining room took forever, having to walk at an incredibly slow pace. Finally, I complained about the heat to Maharishi.

"You want air conditioning?" he asked right away. God, he was still treating me like a little diva! No one else had air conditioning in their rooms, but after I spent a brief moment considering what kind of problems that might create, I said yes. An air conditioner was ordered from New Delhi and soon thereafter installed in my room. But the electricity was knocked out shortly afterward for an extended time, so I don't think I ever actually got to use it before we left.

Even though the heat and the dysentery were wearing me down, the thought of leaving "Maharishi's world" in this vast and mystical country also made me anxious. Our next point of arrival would be Livigno, Italy, a ski resort high in the Alps near the Italian/Swiss border. An international seminar had been organized at a hotel there so that Maharishi could meet with as many of the 500 thus far trained teachers of meditation as possible. At the same time I knew that as soon as we left India Maharishi would meet the renowned Jemima again, the woman whom everyone said was so special to Maharishi. What was it about this woman that gave her such a strong influence over him? I was both envious of her power and curious about who she was. Young and insecure, I lacked the confidence to relax and just be myself, wanting to be more like that special woman in the belief that Maharishi would love me more. So I started to nag him about taking silence, thinking I should be more like "Ma":

*"Maharishi—*

*1) You are the originator, the inspiration, the crux, the figurehead of the spiritual regeneration movement.*

*2) It is absolutely essential that you remain well rested, fresh, alert, and healthy at all times.*

*3) The degree of activity is directly proportional to the degree of rest.*

*4) You must set a good example for all meditators and course members by practicing what you preach.*

*5) Please take some silence today.*

*Jai Guru Dev*

*Love, Judith"*

He wrote back on the same paper:

*"Sweet is your thought dear Judith. I am sure this should be so. I will try, yes. Enjoy."*

This note makes me laugh at myself. I can see my insecurity in trying to be like someone else. At the same time, I did have a genuine concern for his well-being. For those of us who had the opportunity to closely observe his lifestyle, it seemed as though he *never* meditated! He was always in action. I heard later that several of the Skin Boys would complain about not being able to stay awake as long as Maharishi could.

What does that mean? Is this a part of enlightenment? I don't know...sometimes I think human beings are like light bulbs, no one is less of a light bulb than another. But some of us are 25 watt bulbs, others 60 watt, a few are 100 watt light bulbs, and then if you are working with photography, you need 1000 watt light bulbs. Maharishi must have been a 1000 watter.

At any rate, the course schedule was set. If a conference or training program was planned, it was a matter of adjusting one's life around those dates. I found comfort in knowing that at least he wanted me to be there.

The day before we were to leave it occurred to me that spending time alone with Maharishi would probably be much more difficult once we left the Ashram. I put my saree and makeup on meticulously as usual and wandered over toward his house. As luck would have it, I found him sitting alone, looking out at the view through the large glass windows of his living room and sat down on the carpeted floor in front of him.

**I started to nag Maharishi about taking silence.**

MAHARISHI—

(1) YOU ARE THE ORIGINATOR, THE INSPIRATION, THE CRUX, THE FIGURE-HEAD OF THE SPIRITUAL REGENERA-TION MOVEMENT. (2) IT IS ABSOLUTELY ESSENTIAL THAT YOU REMAIN WELL RESTED, FRESH, ALERT, AND HEALTHY AT ALL TIMES. (3) THE DEGREE OF ACTIVITY IS DIRECTLY PROPORTIONAL TO THE DEGREE OF REST. (4) YOU MUST SET A GOOD EXAMPLE FOR ALL MEDITATORS AND COURSE MEMBERS BY PRACTISING WHAT YOU PREACH. (5) __PLEASE TAKE SOME SILENCE TODAY.__

JAI GURU DEV

LOVE, JUDITH

Sweet is your thought dear Judith. I am sure this should be so. I will try, yes. Enjoy.

"So, tomorrow we leave," I said.

I could see an expression of discomfort on his face.

"What's the matter, Maharishi?"

"I don't want to go," he said, punctuating his sentence with a small, spitting sound of disgust. "I want to stay here in India, with you."

I was quite taken. I saw his anxiety about traveling back into the West and also had a dread of my own. At the same time, I basked in the warmth of this expression of intimacy. I didn't know what to say, so I didn't say anything. We just sat there, facing each other in silence. Unexpectedly, someone else came into the room, and this special moment was over.

I have often reflected over the resistance he was feeling about leaving India at that time. Maharishi would still have 38 more years to spread his knowledge and successfully expand his movement, building up a multi-billion dollar organization. And yet, in many ways, during those years he would lose more and more of his innocent interaction with various members of his ever changing inner circle. There would be more clandestine affairs with young women in the movement; there would be court cases involving the use of funds; there would be life-threatening sabotage, and during the last years of his life he would become filled with paranoia directed at some of his closest devotees, and completely isolate himself from the world.

Maharishi with other holy men and Western devotees in India.

# Mantras in the Alps

Once we arrived at the airport in Zurich, Switzerland, we had several hours of extra time before the next leg of our journey toward Livigno, Italy. I booked a shower room and delighted in the luxury of plenty of warm water in a bathroom with floors that had been meticulously washed and polished. In contrast to India, everything about Switzerland was clean and neat. Even their wood piles were stacked in obsessively tidy rows, which could be seen from our car windows as we were driven through beautiful landscapes in cars arranged by devotee Count Blücher.

My body was grateful to be out of India. After so many weeks of dysentery and the itching rash from my one-sided diet of mangoes, I had become quite physically weak. In desperation I decided to go to an Indian pharmacy in Delhi just before our departure.

The pharmacist took one look and said, "You need a shot of antihistamine. Please go over there and remove your underwear."

Oh my God! Back behind the curtain, down with my pants, and up with my white western fanny in front of this dark skinned stranger who was not even supposed to look at women's uncovered legs. Thankfully he was very professional, and the antihistamine started working immediately. My body was on the road to recovery.

I was leaving that all behind me now as we sped through the countryside, our cars climbing higher and higher, high enough so you could feel the pressure change in your ears. I had never seen anything

Livigno, Italy, in the Alps near the Swiss border.

so breathtaking...there were places where we were surrounded by green fields, flowers and trees and yet in the not too far distance we could see snow-capped mountains at the same time.

One thing I have to say about following Maharishi around the world for two years was that I also got to travel to many of our planet's most lovely places.

**Our group has just arrived in Livigno, June 1970. What a contrast after months of dust and dysentary! Judith in the forefront.**

After a couple of days at the conference hotel which had been rented off-season at the Livigno ski resort, I could see that there was an immediate difference as to how accessible Maharishi was. Roughly 300 of his then 500 trained teachers of Transcendental Meditation had come from all corners of the world to be with their beloved master, and many of them

From Rishikesh, India to Livigno, Italy I was dressed in a lilac version of the silk chiffon sarees that Maharishi was so fond of.

This was one of the earliest international gatherings of TM teachers. There were only 500 in total at the time.

I'm sitting in the audience, to the right in the photo.

© Theo Fehr

© Theo

That's Johannes Olivegren on the right in the photo, relaxing outside the conference hotel. Conny Larsson is sitting to his left.

wanted a private interview. I hadn't seen Maharishi for what seemed like an eternity (maybe three days), and was trying to handle my frustration over the new wall of separation. In India, I had been in the habit of presenting him with garlands of flowers that were easily bought at nearby markets. But in Livigno there were no flower markets, only shops with very expensive cut flowers. I remember taking a long walk in the area surrounding the hotel and being delighted to find an abundance of a species of yellow water lily growing wild beside a brook. They could be used for a garland! As I write this, it amazes me that I could live on moments like this for so long, happy to thread the blossoms of these flowers into a necklace that I would later place around his neck. This would give me the oppor-

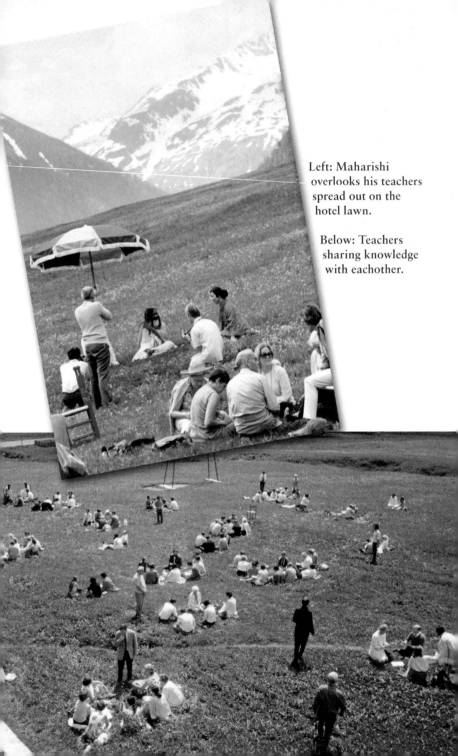

Left: Maharishi overlooks his teachers spread out on the hotel lawn.

Below: Teachers sharing knowledge with eachother.

tunity to, in spite of being in the midst of a crowd of devotees, get within inches of his physical body.

Maharishi would soon start the conference with a lecture on what he had coined as "The Science of Creative Intelligence." This was the beginning of a new chapter in how he would present meditation to the world, and the first time that he made sure his lectures would be videotaped. (Maharishi must be one of the most videotaped gurus in the world. I have a huge box of sound tapes that Johannes recorded every time he was with him.) We, his trained teachers, were sitting together, waiting for him to come and ascend his white "throne."

Where ever he went, the spot from which he lectured was prepared in advance by devotees in the same way... a chair covered with white cloth and a large picture of Guru Dev behind him, as well as plenty of floral arrangements, lit candles and sometimes incense if it was allowed. Everyone had their defined roles around him...the Flower Girl, or the Skin Boy, his Secretaries, or his Private Cook. Beyond room and board, no one was ever paid for these roles. This was volunteer work at the highest level...it was regarded as an extreme honor to be allowed to serve the guru in some specific way, and everyone performed their tasks with love and devotion. This is a part of the Hindu tradition in India: the guru is taken care of and nourished by those who follow him. In exchange, devotees hope for their guru's blessings and knowledge which they believe will assist them to reach a state of enlightenment.

When Maharishi finally walked into the room, I

Another meditation teacher got a quick shot of me as I ran by him in my white silk chiffon saree.

Conny Larsson on the left in photo, Berndt Högberg on the right.

noticed a woman with simply cut, straight brown hair walk in just behind him at the same time. This must be Jemima I thought, and studied her carefully. She was much younger than I had expected, perhaps in her early forties? With a nickname like "Ma" I had imagined a stoutly, gray haired woman. She had a very pleasant countenance and radiated a quiet, for lack of more inventive words, strength and goodness. The meeting I had dreaded was suddenly over and hadn't been horrible at all...in fact, in spite of envying her position, I liked Jemima very much from the very start. During Livigno I would also meet two other persons who would take on significant roles later in my life. One was an architect within Maharishi's inner circle of favorites, Johannes Olivegren, and another was Conny Larsson, who had become a teacher of meditation during the 1969 Teachers' Training course in India. They were both from Sweden.

The course in Livigno was the beginning of a new kind of life with Maharishi. If I had realized it fully then I would most likely have been very unhappy, because the quiet, intimate days in India with a small group of devotees and plenty of private moments were over forever. But I was still living off my recent experiences from Rishikesh, and momentarily distracted by the impending visit from two important members of my biological family.

My parents had never been to Europe, which is something most Americans feel the need to do, and when friends invited them to make the trip together they took the chance to check up on me at the same

I am sitting with my back toward the camera in a white shawl. Jerry Jarvis on the left.

time. I had a private moment with Maharishi in preparation for their arrival. The plan was that I would teach them to meditate during their stay.

Maharishi said to me,

"Give your father xxxx as the mantra he should use."

"But Maharishi, that's the mantra we usually give to students," I questioned.

Maharishi had taught us to give out our mantras on the basis of, amongst other things, age.

"Yes, but your father is an intellectual man. He will enjoy that mantra."

"What about the effects of the next mantra?"

"That is a good mantra for people who are building their careers."

"And the next?"

"Good for the time of life when you can enjoy success."

"And the last?"

"Rest."

The memory of this private conversation has stayed with me all these years. You see, Maharishi was never, at least during my training, very open about the mantras he gave us to use—their actual meaning, or their specific effects. He told us that they came from the Vedas, ancient knowledge that had been cognized by rishis (seers) who had channeled this information from divine sources. Originally the four chapters of the Vedas had been passed on through oral tradition but were eventually written down in Sanskrit and contain hymns and incantations that are thousands of years old.

Left: Here is Maharishi on one of his favourite outings...looking at possible sites for meditation academies.

Below: The inner circle always wanted to go along on a land hunt. Judith with a white shawl.

We had been trained to say that the mantra was to be used without any consideration as to its meaning... that it worked on a sound vibration level, and that was it. And yet the conversation I had just had with him implied that specific mantras did in fact create specific effects.

At the time, I was too young and inexperienced to notice it, but in later years it seemed that his selection of which mantras to use for the different age groups came out of his own value system as to what was important for all human beings at various stages of their lives.

The rest of the time in Livigno was spent pleasantly, going to lectures and sharing new procedures with the other teachers out on the lawns. I remember feeling excited over being able to start to apply some of the training we had just completed and felt so competent.

The other memory I have from the few weeks we spent there is that the architect, Johannes Olivegren, took an interest in me, but at the time there was only one man I was interested in...Maharishi Mahesh Yogi.

# Poland Springs

The next stop on this particular world tour was Poland Springs, Maine where Maharishi was holding a course during the month of July 1970. I had spent some time with my parents in their new home in Florida where my father was teaching psychology at the University of Gainesville. Mother had stopped teaching and seemed to be satisfied in her role as a dutiful housewife and was enjoying decorating their new home.

As soon as I could manage it, I was back with Maharishi at Poland Springs. There were even more people here than in Livigno, and I started to feel a little lost. Donning Maharishi's favorite silk saree when I returned from Florida, as well as the gold bracelets on my arm, I remember coming into a room where a group of about 40 people sat on the floor in complete silence hanging onto every word from the master. In this outfit, any physical movement was accompanied by a kind of swishing, jingly sound, so you could hardly miss my entrance. Maharishi looked up and I noted that he knew I was there.

Day to day life here was different from day to day life in Livigno. I performed my very first TM initiations and was so excited! I also started working with various secretarial tasks since I could type and had good verbal skills, and there was a need to have some excuse to be around Maharishi.

At that time Jerry Jarvis was the man who was closest to Maharishi. He headed the huge US branch of the Students' International Meditation Society that was expanding with leaps and bounds since the involvement of the Beatles and other famed celebrities.

Jerry did not want me to wear sarees. He thought that we could be too easily labeled "sect." Trying to cooperate, I put on a Western dress and wore it in front of Maharishi for the first time. Jerry and Maharishi were sitting alone out on a veranda at the hotel. I had brought a camera with me from home since it finally occurred to me that I ought to take some pictures of my own of Maharishi. I could have taken hundreds of pictures of him, but the ones you see here are among the few that I ever took.

I never thought these pictures were any good. They were packed away somewhere, and I came across them when looking through old material in researching this book. Today I see them with very different eyes. I realize there is something of value here...they are so personal. He looks a little shy and embarrassed. I remember standing in front of him saying, "Maharishi... Maharishi..." trying to get him to look at the camera. I had undoubtedly disturbed them in the middle of their talk—you can see that he has had to put his pen down. But I was determined. Now or never I thought. I knew that this was the first time he had seen me in a short, Western dress but was only focused on getting the pictures. As soon as I took them, I left, aware that I had walked out to them unannounced.

Shortly after, Maharishi met with me and told me that he did not want me to wear Western clothes. I explained that Jerry did not want me to wear sarees anymore now that we were out of India. Maharishi insisted, so I went back to sarees when I was around him.

After Poland Springs, the memories are more blurred. I was with Maharishi at Humboldt, California, Amherst, Massachusetts, Boulder, Colorado, and Estes Park, Colorado. We traveled constantly, and our living environment at various hotels and conference centers was changing all the time. I also worked at a TM center in Berkeley, California for a time, as well as on three different Mallorca courses, but it is difficult to remember in what order I was where. Sometime during all of this it was decided that I would become Jerry's private secretary, which would entail trips to Los Angeles, California to the SIMS head office. I remember being somewhat perplexed about my new job.

I could have taken *hundreds* of pictures of Maharishi, but these are among the very few that I took. We are in Poland Springs, Maine, USA, seven months into our love affair. Maharishi looks a little shy and embarrassed. That could be because this is the first time he has seen me in a short Western dress...my legs are showing!

I had said to Maharishi, "But when will I be with you?"

His reply: "When Jerry comes, you come."

I couldn't tell whether Maharishi wanted me out of his hair or whether he was assuring that we could be together without raising suspicion. Now I think it was probably a little of both. Perhaps he was already beginning to tire of my undying devotion. Later I learned more about his relationships with other women, and it

Jerry holding blankets, me in the background, and Maharishi clutching some wild flowers I gave him just moments before Johannes took this picture. We are in Switzerland.

seems as if he wanted to do the chasing. Now and then I would see a woman actively trying to seduce him, but my impression is that he wanted to keep that sort of behavior at a distance.

But I did enjoy working for Jerry whom I found to be intelligent, responsible and devoted with a deep spirituality. At the same time, he was not a wuss, and actually dared to voice an opinion of his own around Maharishi. Working for Jerry meant dressing Western style, so eventually I was able to phase out the sarees altogether.

# The Bubble Cracks

Bit by bit I noticed that I was no longer the favorite, or you could say that I finally allowed all outer signs to sink in. He did not seem as delighted to see me and stopped asking me to come to him at night. My last night with him was at some hotel in Mallorca; it was sweet but the needy passion was gone from his side. I could see his interest in other young women and guessed that he was most likely spending intimate time with them, even though I didn't have proof of the latter.

Once I saw a lovely German girl sitting and waiting by his door at one of the Teachers' Training courses in Mallorca. My room was right across from his, so it was easy to see comings and goings. A moment later

I'm busy with some secretarial task on Mallorca, Course I or II. That is Ned Wynn and Jerry Jarvis in the background.

I was on my way to the elevator and happened to run into her. She had just left Maharishi and was crying, but obviously did not want to talk about it. That unnerved me. A day or so later I was in with him, asking what was going on...were they having a love affair? He became irritated with me. How could I think such a thing?

"She wants to become a Brahmacharini!" he said. (This is the Hindu version of a Christian nun...).

He didn't like me pressing him on the issue, and this was perhaps the beginning of my "downfall" as a member of the inner circle. I was still Jerry's secretary at that time, but today, according to reports from various skin boys and other involved persons, I am quite sure that Maharishi had already initiated physical contact with other young women.

I remember one of these turning up on one of the Mallorca courses. She was not dressed in a saree, but in a long, puffy dress that looked out of place...as though she had walked straight out of a Victorian film. This could have been her own device, not wanting to appear as though she was a member of a sect by wearing an Indian saree, and yet wanting to respect Maharishi's wishes that she not expose her legs. She had just arrived, and even though there were many around us, I saw how pleased he was when she came walking toward him in the corridor. He said something in a low voice to her, and she put her face quite near his to hear what he was saying. I saw her focus, catching every word, and then a slight nod of the head, with a beaming smile. They had just made an agreement that she would come to him in the night. I knew the signals.

Suddenly I could see the whole situation objectively. *"My happiness is completely dependent upon whether or not I spend time with Maharishi, and whether or not I feel loved or appreciated by him,"* I thought. *"This is not healthy. This is not going to lead to a happy life. I have to leave."*

So many times I've wished that I had already been trained in emotional therapeutic work when I realized I needed to leave Maharishi. The pain that welled up in me was excruciating, and I had no one I could talk to about it. I remember sitting alone in my room in Mallorca, just beating my chest harder and harder to help the pain to come out. I cried and cried and cried. The only one who may have noticed that I was not in good shape would have been Jerry, whom I still worked for.

You could say, that it was the equivalent of having to go through a divorce for a woman who has discovered that her partner has been unfaithful. Of course, no such marriage existed, except in my heart. I had planned to stay with Maharishi for the rest of my life, in a role that would have been some kind of self-imposed mixture of being his lover/nun. All parts of me—the woman, the inner child, the devotee—had trusted him so deeply, so openly, so naively. That was why the decision to leave was very tough. Not only would I have to leave him as a lover, I would also have to leave him as my teacher. At that time I still believed Maharishi was the only connection to knowledge from a divine source on the planet, and leaving that aspect of him was just as difficult as leaving the man that I loved.

The inner circle dines with MMY at someone's private home in Switzerland. Look at Maharishi...the contrast between this man's level of power and the size of his body is, well, humorous! I am sitting on the left in the picture, Jerry is to the left of Maharishi, and Johannes Olivegren is on the right.

The golden bubble of being so loved, so nurtured, and so protected that Maharishi had built up around me burst into a million pieces, and I was left to face all of the fears and feelings of abandonment that I still carried with me from my childhood. I wish I had known that much of the pain came from unhealed experiences from the past, but I didn't. I thought it only had to do with what was happening in the now, and felt absolutely heart broken.

The agreement of secrecy concerning our relationship only made things worse. Being in a prison of silence, along with the constant traveling and the jealousy between staff members all added up to pretty solid isolation. I don't know how I managed to get through this period without talking to someone about it, but I did.

# The Beginning
## of the End

I walked across the hall to Maharishi's room one day at one of the hotels where we stayed. The door was open, so I went in. He had just left and in a bit of a hurry, because his hair brush was still lying on the middle of the bed. A part of me must have already known that I was planning to leave, because when I saw his hair collected in the brush, I knew what to do...I wanted a momento and took it. But still, the decision to leave him turned out to be a rather long, drawn out process for me. Thankfully he was not actively kicking me out...I was still around him via the inner circle up to the last months. Yet having been so intensely wrapped up in him and his movement had cut my ties with any-

Johannes Olivegren greets Maharishi at the airport in Malmö, Sweden, 1967. I had met neither of them yet.

thing that would provide any kind of backup. Nor had I confided in my parents. So the prospect of throwing myself out into the "real world" without a job or a home, without a purpose, without close friends, and without Maharishi as my anchor, frightened me into indecision and passivity.

As my intimate meetings with Maharishi were phasing out, my relationship with Johannes Olivegren, the man who would later become my life partner and the father of my only child, started phasing in. He was an appreciated member of Maharishi's inner circle and would show up now and then.

Johannes was a handsome, charming and successful architect from Sweden. Since Maharishi was always planning new academies all over the world, he loved to sit and talk with Johannes about these plans. I remember driving around Switzerland with him since

140

Maharishi had asked him to find a place that he could use as a base for the movement's international headquarters. That he did, and the choice landed on Grand Hotel Sonnenberg located at one of the most beautiful spots in the world, Seelisberg, Switzerland.

The view from this hotel was and is absolutely stunning. Lake Luzern lies straight below in a long, deep drop and looking across the lake from the grounds one sees beautiful, high mountains. These geographical conditions often created a dramatic effect of fog in the morning that would gradually dissipate as the sun came up. Once I saw a double rainbow there that was so intensely bright you would have thought you could reach out and touch it.

It was at Seelisberg that Johannes and I began to fall in love, and I remember breaking out in sobs as I allowed another man to get physically close with me. I felt I had to explain my reaction, and that's how he became the first person that I could talk to about my relationship with Maharishi. He was also clever and mature enough to not start creating dramatic scenes about the whole thing...I think he had been around during the whole hullabaloo concerning Mia Farrow. We agreed that we would keep the whole thing to ourselves for the time being, and for me it was a tremendous relief to have someone to talk to.

But Johannes was a married man, with children. As I look back on that part of my life, I deeply regret the hurt that my entrance on the scene must have inflicted on his lovely wife and children, and had I been mature enough to understand what I was getting involved

Above: The site of a possible TM academy in Switzerland.
Below: Johannes would have his office make up a model of
the envisioned academy.

Above: Maharishi cruising from above in the search for land.
Below: Maharishi is looking at a possible house type for the
planned academy. Jemima Pitman in the background. Vernon
Katz and Angelika von Kirchen in the photo as well.

with, I would have made other decisions. Another aspect of this situation was that Johannes was not completely honest with me about his situation at home. Be that as it may, as time went on, and the circumstances became more and more dramatic as to how and when I would extract myself from Maharishi and his movement, the relationship with Johannes became a lifeline for me to hang onto.

Johannes and I planned to meet at the 1972 Teachers' Training course on Mallorca. I felt that this would be a good time to finalize my relationship with Maharishi, and try to get his blessings for my relationship with Johannes. In the beginning, he had been observing our growing attraction for each other rather passively, but as time went on he started actively to try and separate us. As I was making plans to travel to Mallorca from Switzerland, Maharishi wrote me a letter from the hotel where he was already installed. In it he tried to talk me out of my plans to go to Sweden to be with Johannes:

*My dear blessed Judith*            *October 10, (71)*

*Jai Guru Dev.*

*I received your telegram but not yet letter. What I have gather(ed) from the air (is) that your persisting sickness has caused a great deal of instability in your thinking. I advised you to get yourself properly treated in the States by experts and for that I had asked Xxxxx to keep on sending expenses as you need. Instead of do-*

*ing that you depended on Johannes. He is a good man but it is a mirage for you. He is not in a position to take responsibility and it is not good for you to think of giving him your responsibility. Take him to (he means 'as') a good friend as I had advised you in the beginning but do not try to build castle in the air.*

*All this kind of thinking has its basis in your weak health. Neither you should think lack of profound basis for life nor you should depend on Johannes. Get yourself properly treated in the States and then start building your future in the movement or on the basis of marriage with some proper choice. Do not set up ideal choice on a level which is not available on earth.*

*It is better to remain on the practical level. Once you are back to normal health everything will look to be progressive. OK.*

*I have great love for you but when you don't listen how can I help you. So just get well first, and all good will follow.*

*Much love*

*Jai Guru Dev*

*Keep me informed of your progress.*

Thankfully, I was perceptive enough in spite of my young age to realize how manipulative Maharishi was in his letter to me. I had had problems with my digestion since the ice cream episode in India, but he tried to undermine my self-confidence by saying that I was so sick I could not trust my own thinking. This was an all too common response from Maharishi if his women were causing problems for him: you are sick, get therapy. I now realize that his advice to break off the affair with Johannes was in fact good advice, but it did not come from any concern about Johannes being married, and I knew that.

I sensed that Maharishi did not want me to come to Mallorca, but since Johannes and I had already made plans to meet there, I booked my flight anyway. I think the handwritten scribbles on the envelope are possible flight times.

Maharishi's letter to me expressing his disapproval of my relationship with Johannes.

My dear blessed Judith

Jai Guru Dev.

I received your telegram but not yet lett[er]
what I have gather from the air that
your persisting sickness has caused a grea[t]
deal of instability in your thinking.
I advised you to get yourself properly treate[d]
in the States by experts and for that I had
asked _____ to keep on sending expances as
you need. Instead of doing that you depended
on Johanas. He is a good man but it is
a miraj for you. He is not in a position t[o]
take responsibility and it is not good for you
to think of giving him your responsibility.
Take him to a good friend as I had
advised you in the beginning but do
not try to b...d _____ the air.

choice. Do not set up ideal choice
on a level which is not available on
earth. It is better to remain on the
practical level. Once you are back to
normal health everything will look to be
progressive. ok.

I have great love for you but
when you don't listen how can I help
you. So just get well first and all good
will follow.

much love
Jai Guru Dev.

Keep me informed
of your progress.

147

I am including a telegram Maharishi wanted sent to Indira Gandhi as a sample of his handwriting, since he signs the letter "Maharishi Mahesh Yogi". The Beatles were on their way to India to spend 3 months with him at the Ashram. He wanted her to meet them and give them her blessings.

148

*Telegram to Indira Gandhi Prime Minister of India, New Delhi*

*Mother India, your spiritual heritage now is the front page news of the worlds' press due to Beatles being blessed by it. They are coming with me for three months to be in the Academy of Meditation Shankaracharya Nagar, Rishikesh. Would you consider personally blessing them at your residence on arrival in Delhi? A documentary film for world wide release will be made by BBC or other company. Govt of India may appeal to the youth of the world by according them an official reception at the airport on the basis of their being MBE Members of the British Empire.*

*During coming weeks I will be touring Europe. Will be happy to receive your reply care (of) Spiritual Regeneration Movement Foundation of Great Britain, (address)*

*Maharishi Mahesh Yogi*

# Time to Say "Jai Guru Dev"

As I traveled toward Mallorca, I remember having a feeling of impending doom. I was nervous about arriving without Maharishi's blessings and didn't really have a fixed plan. Little did I know that I was about to land in the middle of a soap opera. If this were to be made into something for broadcast, you could call it "spiritual reality TV."

One memory from that course is the entrance of a woman named June. We had met on earlier courses, at Amherst, Massachusetts and Livigno, Italy and were relatively well acquainted with each other. I remember how she would always just knock on my door, plunk herself down on my bed, and hang out whether or not

I was prepared to be social. There she was again, in Mallorca. She started off with a brief moment of small talk. Then suddenly, in a very direct manner, she asked me "Did you xxxx Maharishi?" Her unexpected question knocked me off my feet. I couldn't get a word out and just hung my head in embarrassment. Up to that point the only person I had dared to speak about my relationship with Maharishi was the new love of my life, Johannes.

June didn't have a hard time interpreting my response, and went on to tell me that there was another woman also on the course who had an ongoing, intimate relationship with Maharishi now. I was not surprised at this point but was still reticent to speak about my own situation. I managed to ask June if anything had happened between her and Maharishi. Her reply was that they had not had intercourse, but once when she was sitting alone with him, wearing a low cut top, he reached into her blouse to feel her breasts. Afterwards, he told her not to wear blouses like that anymore.

In the days following this conversation I started to feel a lot of inner turmoil and pretended to "go into silence," a method of not speaking with anyone that is not at all uncommon in spiritual circles. The thought is that by not speaking, one can go within for the purpose of an inner dialogue even though there may be a lot of people around. I think I chose this method to avoid having to talk with anyone outside my room when I was so emotionally unstable.

Maharishi called my room on the telephone.

"Jai Guru Dev!"

"Hello Maharishi."

"How it is?"

"Not very good, Maharishi."

I cannot remember exactly what detail it was that made the dam burst, but suddenly I felt myself become very angry with him. In a clear and firm tone I simply said,

"You know, everything you say when you are up on your podium is true...but when it comes to the people who are closest to you, you treat them like they are little puppets, putting someone here, moving someone there, whatever way you want to."

"No, no, no! The thinking is wrong!" he whined.

"Well, I think the thinking is right!" I said angrily.

I actually hung up on him.

The next day, a friend who had been sitting with Maharishi and others during his evening meal told me that he had been in a very bad mood, and even let out a disgruntled "Women!" as he was eating. At that point, I felt rather satisfied with myself, having dared, finally, to tell the famous guru what I thought of him.

My analogy was quite accurate. Maharishi had his finger in the pie with all of the members of his inner circle. And also with people that he didn't like. Once I overheard him say about someone he found irritating, "Get rid of her." I do not believe for a minute that that statement included planned violence...he just wanted this person out of his space, and would leave it up to other members of the inner circle to handle, washing his hands of the situation.

One or two days later, the other woman involved, Belinda, snuck into my room at night so we could speak openly. Maharishi had ordered one of the Skin Boys to stand outside my door during the day to make sure that I didn't talk to anyone. We both think he was trying to prevent me from telling Belinda that he had also been intimate with me. She tells me now that he was not happy about my plans to come to Mallorca. I don't remember any bad feelings between Belinda and I...rather a sisterhood in being in the middle of a situation that we didn't really know how to cope with. We were both upset with him, for different reasons. She had not realized that Maharishi had been with other women, and I was in the process of trying to figure out how to be with the man I now loved, having in recent months done my best to cut the ties in my heart with my guru. This was the only time she and I really had the freedom to speak with each other in person... now that the proverbial cats were out of the bag, things were happening fast.

I wanted Johannes to come. Recently I found a letter I had written to him from Mallorca that shows my state of mind. I had forgotten how frightened I was:

*"The situation here is very intense. I am unable to speak with you and am unable to tell you in a letter. And so I am just waiting until you get here."*

*"Please come well rested—you will need all of your strength to deal with the intricacy of our situation."*

Mentally and emotionally, I was preparing my departure. A few days after I hung up on Maharishi on the phone, I started to chicken out on my indignant position, thinking that this would most likely be the last time I would be with him. Did I really want those to be my last words? Did I want to leave him in anger? I was still so insecure.

I asked for, and received a private audience. He was lying down, and I gave him a rose and went directly to sit on the floor at the far end of his bed. Guilt ridden, I don't think I said much except to mumble some sort

**This is the letter filled with panic that I sent to Johannes from Mallorca.**

of apology for having been so angry. I didn't mention anything about June or Belinda, not wanting to bring up such an uncomfortable subject. Toward the end of our conversation he just said, "I gave you enough love to last a lifetime..." in a tone of voice that meant I had no right to complain about his behavior.

I just said, "Yes, Maharishi." I was very uncomfortable and wanted to get out of the room. We never said hello or good-bye in the TM movement...we always just said Jai Guru Dev.

"Jai Guru Dev, Maharishi," I said and got up to go.

"Jai Guru Dev," he said as I left. That was the last time I ever spoke with him.

Not long after that Belinda decided to leave Mallorca and escaped with June's help, and June and I wanted out of there as well. I was done. Before she left, June called me and told me that she had told Maharishi that I now knew about his relationship with Belinda. Afterwards, I wondered why she did that. Belinda remembers that I told her Maharishi had in the end said, alright then, go to Sweden. I think he was just happy to see me get out of Mallorca; it wasn't about giving his blessings for the relationship with Johannes. Now he was head over heels in love with the next piece of candy in his box of Western chocolates.

# Poof!

The months after my departure were very difficult emotionally. I had had an affair with a world famous guru and fallen deeply in love. When it was over, I was on the one hand broken hearted and on the other hand bound to secrecy. Talking with my parents was out of the question. I had no residence or work to return to after spending two years of my life traveling with Maharishi and his movement. I had gone from being sure that I would devote my life to him and the spreading of Transcendental Meditation to feeling that the only way to regain balance in my life was to cut all ties. This was a lot for a young woman to handle. I was extremely grateful that Johannes had fallen in love

Johannes Olivegren escorts Maharishi to meet the King of Sweden, 1973.

with me, even though I was conflicted about being attracted to a married man. At the same time, I have to thank Johannes for "saving my life" once I made the decision to leave Maharishi. Psychologically, I leaned heavily on him as I put myself back together, bit by bit. I was not acting suicidal, but certainly felt it at times. I had frequent fits of endless crying and my health really did go downhill.

In the meantime, I was shocked to hear that June had died in a plane crash. The story was that she had gone back to the States and been very upset. I heard recently from an insider that Maharishi had kicked her out of the movement and that she wanted to kill herself. She had called someone she was close to at the Cambridge Center after arriving in North Carolina and sounded hysterical, saying that she had some very upsetting news about MMY and would not discuss any more on the phone. Not long after, she was out with a young man from the movement she was dating, flying to look at new land that had been purchased. It was a clear day with a blue sky. For some, to this day undetermined reason, their plane went down. All 4 persons, June, her companion, another young movement leader, and the pilot were killed. This frightened the wits out of me. I didn't think that Maharishi had technically orchestrated this accident, but I did start to believe that he could obliterate me with his thoughts if he wanted to.

Johannes participated in a previously agreed upon 'Seminar on the Science of Creative Intelligence' with Maharishi in Sweden in 1973 and escorted him to meet the king of Sweden. After that, he decided to make one last trip to Seelisberg in Switzerland. When he returned, he was sure that he would never go back again. About me Maharishi had said, "Remember, a rose has thorns!" He was still trying to break us up. In Sweden, Johannes, in his position as Professor at Chalmers Technical University and head of a successful architectural firm, had often been seen in the newspapers and on television, speaking about the benefits of Transcendental Meditation. Like me, he still loved his meditation and never stopped practicing it, but he completely let go of any public support of Maharishi and his movement.

# Why have I
# Remained Silent?

During the first years of being estranged from Maharishi, I was still so insecure that the thought of "going public" was very frightening. After all, I knew of one girl who had started to talk about Maharishi's escapades far and wide, and she ended up dead shortly thereafter. Better not make a scene I thought. I was so certain of Maharishi's power that I even thought he could be sending me negative energies. It seemed as though wherever I went there was thunder and lightning. I actually believed if Maharishi wanted me out of the way, he could just wish me into oblivion. And yet I didn't dare to speak with anyone about all of this except Johannes, who knew what I had been through.

This is about one year after I have left Maharishi. I'm still wearing the jewelry he gave me.

Now that I had cut myself off from Maharishi and his movement, I searched for other forms of personal development and discovered a school of therapy called Re-evaluation Co-Counseling (RC), a method developed in the USA by Harvey Jackins during the 1950's. I traveled to America to learn more and attended a two-week long workshop with a group of experienced teachers. RC postulates that most of human dysfunction and painful emotions come from thoughts and belief systems held within our minds as a result of unprocessed traumatic childhood experiences and that we should not necessarily base present day decisions in our lives on those feelings.

After deep releases involving a lot of crying, shaking, sweating, and yelling, I became not only more relaxed, but also landed in some very high states of consciousness. By 1974 I was holding the first RC fundamentals class in Sweden, still young and insecure, but the positive aspects of this method were moving me forward. Another of their postulates is that a sense of personal power, as opposed to feeling like a helpless victim, is possible to be reclaimed. Through Co-counseling, I was also able to start building positive relationships with women for the first time in my life.

Another gift from the universe arrived in 1976 through a good friend from England whom I had met within the Co-counseling network. Russel Brown put a book in my hands called "Seth Speaks" written by Jane Roberts. Jane channeled a series of books called the Seth material, and that book led me to another called "The Nature of Personal Reality". If I were to pick one book to recommend to my fellow brothers and sisters on this planet, it would be "The Nature of Personal Reality". This Seth, whoever he-she was-is, writes that no matter what the outer appearance of a situation, even those events which appear very tragic, no one person is ever a complete victim. There is always, preceeding even the most horrendous of situations, a karmic and energetic agreement between the souls involved, and that this is the way it's meant to go down. No one becomes a victim unless he or she has, albeit from perhaps a subconscious or super conscious decision, agreed to take that role upon him or herself.

Something about the way this was written sank in. I started to feel less afraid. Gradually, along with the help from my counseling sessions, I was able to accept this version of reality and stopped seeing myself as someone who could be struck dead from out of the blue. It became more important to start experiencing myself as a co-creator of my universe.

More years passed and I watched the TM movement from a distance. I couldn't believe it when Maharishi was calling some kind of levitation technique "flying" and immediately felt the term was both exaggerated and inappropriate for Western culture that values scientific objectivity. I had often felt in spending so much time around Maharishi that his judgement in terms of how he would market meditation was way out of balance.

Johannes and I used to say to each other that we thought most of the most mature persons who would try to advise him about this sort of thing were blatantly ignored, and then we noticed that they would just sort of phase themselves out. They may have become disillusioned when he would go that far.

Then the price to learn to meditate became sky high...18,000:- in Sweden (2000—3000 dollars depending on the rate of exchange). Once again, I was shocked. I had started to teach meditation again, but did not market myself as a TM teacher. With these developments within the movement, whenever mentioning my background and training to clients I started to say, "In case you have heard strange things about the TM movement, I want to tell you that the meditation technique is one thing, and how Maharishi runs his movement is another. Please keep them separate."

When I finally heard that Maharishi was charging $1,000,000 for his enlightenment program, I felt like he had gone off the deep end, and couldn't believe that people would actually pay him that much money.

While reading about these various developments I'd usually think, "If they only knew..." But in the end would always come to the conclusion that Maharishi was doing more good in the world than harm, and continued to stay silent.

# I Find a Brother

Once I had left Maharishi, I made no attempt to come back within the fold, so I have no personal experience of what developed in terms of his relationships with women later on. However, in 2002, I would reconnect with another former TM teacher who had also been a part of the inner circle surrounding Maharishi, Conny Larsson. The next time Conny and I met we would have a lot of catching up to do.

Johannes and I had given birth to a son in 1978, Jonathan. This was his fifth child and my only child. When Jonathan was old enough to go to daycare, I went back to university to start a new profession as a filmmaker and editor and free-lanced at Swedish

Inset: Our son Jonathan, born 1978.
Johannes and I, later in life...1986.

Television for many years. My third documentary "Sowing for Need or Sowing for Greed?" was broadcast in March 1989[4].

About five months later, Johannes died suddenly of cancer, only two weeks after we had discovered his illness. A debilitating depression followed. In a sense, this was the first time I stood truly alone, without having the love of a strong man to help me feel safe. Fortunately, I was able to recover through healing myself on deeper levels and also by training within yet another school of human development, shamanism. In total, it took about four or five years to come back fully to life.

---

4 Sowing for Need or Sowing for Greed?"—My documentary about genetically modified seeds. It was awarded a Gold Dukat at the 1989 Mannheim Film Festival, as well as the Audience Prize. Swedish title: "Draksådd".

I had met Conny Larsson in 1970 in Livigno, Italy at the first international TM teachers' conference, but we didn't have much contact with each other back then. He'd become a TM teacher during the 1969 training course in India. Now, in 2002, without having spoken with or seen each other for several decades, we were both traveling around from area to area within Sweden, giving different courses. Often I would hear, "Oh, Conny Larsson was just here, teaching meditation." I understood from what people described that Conny was teaching meditation in a different manner than the way he had been trained by Maharishi. He called it Vedic Mantra Meditation instead. I was curious about what kind of changes he had made but was never motivated enough to get in touch with him. Not until a woman named Bima Andén and I happened to be giving courses at the same center in Värmland, Sweden.

Bima and I were taking a long walk in the beautiful grounds around the center. As we shared our backgrounds, I mentioned that my first occupation after university was as a teacher of TM and that I had worked as a personal secretary to Maharishi Mahesh Yogi. She then told me that her friend Conny Larsson had also worked closely with Maharishi and that Conny was writing a book about his experiences with Sai Baba, the guru that he went to after he had left Maharishi.

Sai Baba and Conny had been lovers for a long time, but it was first now that he had decided to come out with his experiences. The moment I heard this I felt,

Conny Larsson attending the 1969 Teachers' Training Course in Rishikesh 1969. Conny at the far right in the picture. He later went on to work for Maharishi as skin boy, masseur, and personal secretary.

"Conny must be someone who understands what I experienced" and decided finally to call him up on the telephone, this man who had been leaving his tracks around me for years.

Back home I called the number Bima gave me. "Hi, Conny. This is Judith Bourque. Do you remember me?" "Of course, I remember you," said Conny. We met in Stockholm shortly thereafter and spent the greater part of an afternoon together sharing what had happened to us since Livigno. Now, decades later, I made up my mind that I would speak with Conny about what had happened between Maharishi and me. In the past, I had been pretty tight lipped about my experiences. Johannes knew of course, and a few other close friends, but I had always asked them to keep our conversation confidential.

Conny said that the moment he heard my voice over the phone, the dime dropped. He had followed Maharishi for ten years, working closely with him between 1972—76. During an extended period as nighttime Skin Boy and personal masseur, he had been asked to leave the key to Maharishi's room to this lady or that lady once or twice a week after Conny had finished giving him his evening massage. He'd believed whatever story had been told him—that they were handling mail, working with some artwork, or some other vague reason and not given it much more thought.

Since then Conny and I have a special understanding for each other, having both been in love with and been loved by our gurus. We made, and survived, the journey of first experiencing what it was like to be "made special" by someone we thought was God personified and then getting psychically mauled by a jolting wake up call. And we both had been asked to keep it secret. In Conny's case, it took 21 years before his eyes opened, and when they did he had to face the fact that his guru, Sathya Sai Baba, the love of his life, was a pedophile charlatan[5].

In my case, I left my guru after only two years of being by his side and could feel, upon regaining personal balance, that Maharishi still had many redeeming features as a teacher of meditation. And I think I am lucky that our relationship took place in the early years of the movement. It sounds like he got much more complicated further down the road.

---

5 "Behind the Mask of the Clown", Conny Larsson's autobiographical account.

# Maharishi Comes to Me in a Dream

One of the tools of my spiritual development over the years has been the use of dreams as an expanded state of consciousness in order to receive spiritual and practical guidance. From keeping a record of my dreams since 1986 and observing the interaction between what happens in the dream state and what happens in everyday reality, I noticed that I would often dream of future events, or pick up useful extra sensory information for family members, friends and clients. A few dramatic examples of what I have experienced is that I dreamt of

This *was* the breakfast room at our hotel. I had had one day of relaxation before the Tsunami hit us.

the 9/11 terrorist attack two weeks before it happened, the 2004 Tsunami one week before it happened, and Princess Diana's death the night that it happened. Dreaming of future events is particularly convincing as to the extra-sensory power of the dream state, since that is not something one can talk oneself into.

The Tsunami dream is a fascinating example. I had planned a trip to India in December 2003 but rebooked my ticket in order to spend Christmas with my son, his partner, her older son and my little granddaughter of one and a half years who were spending the winter in Thailand. The new ticket turned out to be horribly uncomfortable and would mean flying in five different airplanes over three days with no single night on the ground. I doubted I would have the physical stamina to make that trip, and asked for spiritual guidance as I fell asleep. That night I had a dream that there would soon be an earthquake and that water levels would rise. I woke up in a cold sweat, knowing not exactly when or exactly where, but I did know that it was going to be soon and somewhere where I had planned to go. This warning helped me make up my mind. If something terrible was going to happen, I wanted our family to be together, not apart! With new motivation I made the grueling trip, falling asleep in the fifth airport. Someone who worked for the airlines woke me up and dragged me out to the last plane. The wave came a day and a half later and my granddaughter was in the ocean with her mother just fifteen minutes before. Obviously we all survived, and I was so grateful to be there to help my children with a number of practical issues as we were rushed off to safety by the hotel personnel. Experiences like this are the reason I pay such close attention to my dreams.

About a year and a half before Maharishi died, I had an unexpected dream that contained the seed of my decision to finally speak out. I hadn't thought about him in a long time, having put our relationship in the category of "past is past." It was a great surprise to dream about him, and to see it all in such detail.

This was the dream:

*I found myself standing in Maharishi's bedroom, directly in front of him. He appeared as I remembered him, except that his legs were as thin as sticks and looked completely emaciated (I have heard that this was, in fact, so during his latter years). He looked quite startled to see me standing there in front of him, but didn't say anything. Instead, he walked over to the left side of the room where a wooden, stand-up closet was placed, rather old-fashioned in style. He opened the double doors of the closet and revealed the inside of it which was pitch black. He then started to climb into the closet, but turned toward me and asked, "Are you going to leave me in the dark?" After he asked me that, I suddenly saw myself standing behind him, dressing him in a fresh set of his white silk robes, the Brahmachari dhotis that he wore throughout his life. As I put the robes over his shoulders, I said, "I have never done this before."*

End of dream. Short, simple, and intensely clear.

Because of having worked with this subject for decades, I know that it can sometimes take a long time to completely integrate the meaning of an important dream. The first part seemed obvious, and yet it felt as though the closet had a double meaning. As he was climbing into the darkness, I thought it represented him climbing into the coffin of death. But it was more than that. What do we keep in closets? Our clothes. In dreams, our clothes can represent the roles we are playing in the film of our lives...as well as they do in this reality. As soon as we see a man dressed in black clothes with a small, stiff white collar we know, without any verbal explanation, that that person is working as a priest. Nurses often dress in white clothes in many cultures. Today medical people are often dressed in light green garb. So when he asked me if I was going to keep him in the dark, he was asking whether or not I was going to let the truth about his role as a celibate monk out of the closet.

The second part of the dream had me stumped. I was dressing him in clean silk dohtis...what did that mean? I put the question on hold.

During the spring of 2009, I started to hear rumors that a German filmmaker was making a documentary on Maharishi. Conny warned me that David Sieveking, the director of the film, might get in touch and ask for an interview and that I needed to think through whether or not to do it.

I was still unsure...and yet now that Maharishi had passed over, I was more open to a possible change. I decided to have a session with an excellent trance channel with whom I have consulted before. These days I am careful about consulting mediums since it can be very addictive to slide into relying too much on someone else's advice. Today if I consult a medium, firstly, I choose this person with care and secondly, approach it with the attitude "let's just see if there is a different angle to this situation...let's get a second opinion before making a decision."

# Consulting a Medium

Those of you who believe in the power of dreams, channeled readings, re-incarnation, karma, etc. may find this session interesting. All of what I just mentioned is, in fact, part of my world view. (That doesn't mean that I expect it to be a part of yours.) I am including these notes, transcribed from an audio recording of the session which was conducted in May, 2009. I have added some comments in brackets to clarify what the medium is referring to.

*Judith:* So the primary thing today is this documentary about Maharishi...a German man named David is working on a documentary about Maharishi, and he wants to do an interview with me. He is hoping I will speak about my relationship with Maharishi. In other words, he is hoping that I will reveal that Maharishi was not a monk. So you have been advising me earlier not to speak of this, and I want to hear your opinion.

*Medium:* Now it is time to divide the Maha and the Rishi...there is a difference, eh? Maha means the great Rishi. Many can be Rishi...

*Judith:* "Seer"...

*Medium:* There is a time for everything, and there is a time for truth. (Looks off into the distance for a moment and is quiet.) I am watching the gate he went through.

There is a time for truth from two points of view: one, to secure the truth about him...the Rishi. And then, there's one truth also for the world that has to be declared. He is coming from a very holy line, a holy lineage and by the way he acted, he broke that lineage.

(But) he was still a Rishi. But he was told, he was told... You see, there are many aspects around this master and there is a man there who has very good intentions for truth. I think it would be good, since truth is truth, and the truth will never hurt. It will just broadcast for the lineage and purification of the lineage. That lineage already from the beginning warned him and said not to participate in this world out there. But he (MMY) had such a force. That was the force that he brought from his master. His master (Guru Dev) was one of the upholders, the important upholders. He warned him; he told him, because he (MMY) had that idea from the beginning, to go elsewhere. But the master wanted him to stay and do the right action.

He didn't.

So a broadcasting of the truth about the man would give benefit for him in his karma and would be a relief for him since...better to know him as he really was...a human being full of love for everyone. But his main target was that he was full of love for the knowledge. That has to be brought out also. But that man, that young man, he has a good intention. (He is referring to David Sieveking.)

*Judith:* Making the film...

*Medium:* He has a pure intention for the truth. The glorification will not come, but the truth will be there. How good he was, and the weaknesses. He (Sieveking) has no bad intention.

*Judith:* Then the next question would be, if I should reveal my identity? They promised me I could be anonymous. So they would change perhaps the quality of my voice or disguise me.

*Medium:* No, that doesn't need to be.

*Judith:* Should I go out with my identity? (surprised)

*Medium:* You would be very brave. But that is, of course, a choice of yours.

*Judith:* Well, when I look in deep, I say to myself I just want to do, actually, what is right, and in this case it's been difficult for me to think clearly what is right...

*Medium:* Right would be to be you. The right to just be you. Saying how it feels. Being you, being proud to be you, letting all the world know. There was nothing wrong done. What's the wrong with a love affair? Because it was love...

*Judith:* I did feel that we loved each other...

*Medium:* He loved you from the first sight that he laid eyes on you, he loved you. That was his weakness...beauty. All people have weaknesses.

No, I think that your optimal consideration should be the truth and to be proud of what you got from him. You got the right thing, but you also lost it. I can feel the pain. But this is, to love high and lose it, it's a danger. But you have had it in your heart and kept it all the time. And, therefore, also, it has been a very sensitive thing, but it's all there, it's in your heart.

*Judith:* Yes, it hurt when he just moved on, and moved on, and moved on...

*Medium:* That was his sign...he never turned back. He just moved on. That was that master. But that was also his strength...to focus on his knowledge.

*Judith:* Not to get all involved in one relationship...

*Medium:* It was his way of cutting ties that bind.

*Judith:* So he would be focusing on the movement or spreading the meditation?

*Medium:* Now he has totally cut the ties to that organization and the movement. He has nothing to do with it. He would not have anything to do with anyone. He has moved on. He is still a teacher. He will still be a teacher, much more refined and then it's very important that that karma doesn't follow him from behind. So if we can clear that in people's mind then that will settle this karma.

*Judith:* Yes. I think for me, if I just get clear in my own mind what the right thing is. Sometimes it's easy for me to see that, and other times in a situation like this it's more difficult because I feel there are many other dimensions, many other aspects...so I feel confused.

*Medium:* The most important thing is to liberate him. He is going to become a teacher again. He can't have that bag around the neck.

*Judith:* I didn't see it that way, so I'm thankful...I thought you might give me another perspective...

*Medium:* Did I?

*Judith:* Yes, completely new.

*Medium:* It's giving back his love. What he gave to you and now you can give back by taking his karma and transforming that. I told you in the beginning...I told you before that you were the gurus'...what did I say?

*Judith:* You said they put their mark on me.

*Medium:* Yes, the marking lady. You were putting the mark on them, and they were putting the mark on you because of the beauty of your heart and also you came with a beauty of the physical. But then one has to cut the ties. And this particular master has many, so that would not only be a help for him; that would be a help for all the other, in this aspect, only women, that have been his followers, in not exactly the same sense as you, but in the sense of being too close to a recluse. And he was a recluse in the way of focusing on the knowledge.

*Judith:* Very focused.

*Medium:* Yes, and that was making him a recluse even if he didn't succeed being a monk.

No, I think that you have come to the position life brought you to, and now will be the crowning point of being brave, all the way into that. And no one will oppose you in that sense, because they will just show their own ignorance; not only ignorance for love, but ignorance for their own master, because they don't have the knowledge of who he was. He might go on to the "Maha" in the next incarnation, but that depends on his karma, how he can be relieved from karma. So if you relieve him from that thing that the whole world is thinking about, eh? Then he's free! What's the point? Who is not having an affair? Priests, popes, whatever they call themselves.

*Judith:* Then there was the money also. I mean that was his other...problem.

*Medium:* They call him the money guru, eh? That's one sort of a weakness he had. But I would say that he also used money for good. He helped many people. But of course, in the end when all his relatives came around him—that was his second weakness, that he wanted to care for the family, but there were other people who were helped, even if it was never known.

So the money question is...all this planet is money. Everyone is running helter skelter, what do you say. I like him. I like him.

*Judith:* Maharishi?

*Medium:* The Rishi...the Maha he never became. But that was his choice I think. He chose that because he thought love was more than being great. But that was in the beginning...he wanted love.

And he had that world urge, for conquering the world with the knowledge, because he felt the knowledge so strong from his teacher. And his teacher was a real knowledge incarnated.

*Judith:* They called him Guru Dev.

*Medium:* Brahman and Ananda = creator of happiness and that was also the Rishi's thing, to bring happiness to the world because he felt the happiness through his teacher. It is a lineage so beautiful. You can't just see it as pearls...it's strings of wisdom that came through him.

*Judith:* My immune system seems to be so weak. (I have periods of feeling burned out...)

*Medium:* It's not that it's weak, it's that you are withholding. Because you don't let go of the energy. You just have to let go of the love energy in relation to this matter we are talking about-the Rishi-that you're holding back.

*Judith:* Really? You mean that will help me with my health?

*Medium:* Of course, it will, because you are letting things out that you have carried within yourself for so long. You see in the system is also the hurt. Being left. Feeling loved you did, but feeling hurt was never meant to...and that gave you a mark...didn't I call you the marked girl? It's good that you clarify the situation. So just let go. Let the energy flow. And don't fear."

\*\*\*\*\*\*\*\*

Up to this point in time, I had been firmly locked into a position of keeping my mouth shut. Various members of the TM movement, invariably men, would now and then get in touch with me due to rumors they had heard, either by email or telephone, and ask me whether or not Maharishi had kept his vows of celibacy. This situation was always extremely uncomfortable and annoying. Conny had also encouraged me to write about my experiences since he felt that he had done the right thing in coming out with his book about Sai Baba. Finally, after Maharishi died, I had started to reconsider my position, but was still ambivalent.

It was this session that finally tipped the scales. Suddenly I could understand the second half of the dream, the part where I was dressing Maharishi in a fresh set of white silk robes. If I chose to speak out, I would be telling the truth for the first time. A public declaration would clean up the negative karma he had left behind in dying with the lie about his celibacy intact. That in turn would help to prepare him for his next incarnation, where he intends to come back again as a spiritual teacher. I would be assisting, from behind (the past), in dressing him in the purity of his coming role. The whole scenario seemed to be a confirmation of the concept of a divine plan existing for each and every one of us. It amazed me that what had happened between Maharishi and me so long ago could still have so much influence in my life.

The surprise of seeing the whole situation from a different angle meant moving from "no" to "yes" in response to David Sieveking's request for an interview. David had written that he neither wanted to present Maharishi as a complete fraud nor did he want to make him out to be a god. Perhaps his film would provide the right framework for coming out?

One final issue remained: would David and his production company give me the right to approve the final edit of my interview? (Since I am professionally trained as a film editor, I was so very aware of how an interview can be manipulated to communicate something entirely different than was originally intended.) CNN India had contacted me about a year before Maharishi died for an interview, but they refused to give me a contract with that option, so it never happened.

More emails back and forth. Then David's producers gave me a contract I could accept, and I was ready to take the silencer from my mouth. From the time David had sent me his first email to saying yes, several months had passed.

I was booked to teach a course in Shamanic Healing in Germany, so we agreed to meet during that process and do the interview. I met David for the first time in August at the airport in Düsseldorf and liked him immediately. After having cleared away all the energetic debris of whether or not to do the interview, we could now just focus on getting the work done.

Meeting David and his crew was fun. He wanted to understand the other subjects I was teaching and allowed me to introduce him to Shamanic healing. That's why I am dressed the way I am in his film, which is my only real regret about the interview. So little of the course work is shown in my introduction that I pop into the film looking like an aging hippy still stuck in the days of flower power. David, can we do it over again?

# Shades of Grey

*"Some things were perfectly clear,*
*seen with the vision of youth.*
*No doubts and nothing to fear,*
*I claimed the corner on truth.*
*These days it's harder to say I know what*
*I'm fighting for.*
*My faith is falling away; I'm not that sure anymore.*
*Shades of grey wherever I go,*
*The more I find out the less that I know.*
*Black and white is how it should be,*
*But shades of grey are the colors I see."*

**Lyrics from "Shades of Gray," Billy Joel, 1993**

Some followers of Maharishi, because they see him as a Satguru, will simply not believe what is written in this book. They will regard my words as fiction, end of story. The thought that Maharishi could ever lie, act rudely or insensitively, be attached to physical pleasure, have greed, etc. is just impossible for them to take seriously.

But what if my story is true? If it is, then he lied, and he lied about it for at least 38 years that I know of. So how could he lie? I wish I could give you and myself one clear, definitive answer to that question. But like Billy Joel, no matter how hard I try, I can't make it black and white anymore.

From a psychological aspect, I suspect that Maharishi was so young and inexperienced when he asked to be allowed to follow and was accepted into the Ashram of Guru Dev, that he did not know what he was promising away as he took vows to live his life as a celibate. He was probably about 23 years old when he made that choice.

And in becoming the personal secretary/bookkeeper of such a spiritual giant as his divinity Brahmananda Saraswati for 13 years, his days must have been full of enough meaningful activity and high spiritual energy that living the life of a celibate was not that difficult.

There was also the power of example. According to Guru Dev's biography[6], the acclaimed saint would not even allow a woman to be present in his ashram. But when his master died, he was on his own. After a

6  "Life and teachings of Swami Brahmananda Saraswati
Shankaracharya of Jyotirmath" (1941-1953), by Paul Mason.

period of silence in the hills, he came down from the mountains to start his own movement and traveled out in the world where he met women from the West. An Indian man, at least at the time he was raised, and in particular living and working at an Ashram, is not accustomed to seeing women's bare skin. It is both embarrassing and arousing at the same time, even if it is as little as a naked arm or foot. And yet he was constantly surrounded by Western women who behaved inappropriately in the presence of a guru, at least according to his culture.

I saw many examples of this myself. Going back in time, I remember once there was a beautiful young woman named Ria who had sat in front of Brahmachari Satyanand during her personal interview for acceptance into the Teachers' Training program wearing a mini-skirt and no underwear. I didn't see this myself...what I saw was how the young men who were assisting reacted. They came out of the room with their jaws hanging open and told us what had happened. About a year later I met her again. This time she was involved with drawing illustrations of Hatha Yoga for the movement. It was just Maharishi, she and I in the room. As she was discussing her drawings with him, she stretched out her bare leg, pointed her little naked foot and asked Maharishi if this was the correct position for the drawing. I knew him well enough to see that he was both shocked and turned on at the same time. After a moment's silence he said, "Yes, that is correct," and pretended as though nothing inappropriate had just happened. I asked Conny if he had

188

Maharishi's master, Guru Dev Brahmananda Saraswati of Jyotirmath. A young brahmachari Mahesh is in the lower right of the picture.

ever run into this woman during his period of working so closely for Maharishi, and he said that he did. According to him, Maharishi asked to be sure to place her in a building that was quite far away from his.

Nevertheless, once he had tasted the fruit of feminine energy, it seems he could no longer be without it. Since the first edition of this book, I've become aware of many more women whom he had intimate contact with. One of them shared with me by the way that he once said to her he thought all Western women were promiscuous.

I have recently been asked if I think Maharishi felt guilty about not keeping his vows. I know he did, at least in the early years. After our first night together he looked despondent. He sat on his bed, looked off into the distance and complained about his own behavior. This was not a man who was at peace with what he had done. Later on, during the last days of my time with Maharishi, the other woman who revealed that she also had intimate contact with him, told me he believed that someone had died during the Teacher Training courses due to their sexual activities. It is obvious to me that he believed in karma[7] and that he felt he would have to pay for his actions, which he viewed to be wrong.

But in spite of the weight of that belief in karmic consequences, his interest in clandestine relations with female devotees did not diminish. According to accounts from various skin boys who were parked outside the master's door, the number of women and frequency of nightly visits increased during the seventies. It appears

---

7 In Hinduism, karma is the law of cause and effect, and we, as human beings, can use our free will to choose good or evil and suffer the consequences or rewards either in this lifetime or the next.

that he came to peace with his own needs and that the conflict of the early years laid itself to rest in time.

The shortest explanation is simply that he noticed he could get away with it. And in that case he did not need to jeopardize his guru image by admitting that he had broken his vows.

For my part, I don't feel that Maharishi needs to be forgiven for wanting to experience life to its fullest, including an active sex life. I do not believe that there is an inherent conflict between sexuality and spirituality. The difficulty arises within his role as a spiritual leader. Do as I say and not as I do. Any human being who has raised children knows that that doesn't work.

But through the years when trying to understand how he could put himself in this situation, I have tried to put myself in his sandals so to speak. Maharishi was very much a man of his times, and those times were times of change, for all of us. I often reflect on my own upbringing; my Dad didn't teach me how to fix an electrical plug or how to build anything and my grandmother always used to go on and on about the wedding dress she was going to sew for me when I grew up. My parents did not prepare me for life as an economically independent, capable woman moving through the world with a sense of rightness about being there on her own, and the concept of the feminine divine or goddess energy was foreign to me until I started working with shamanism as a middle-aged woman.

Maharishi was raised in a world where men and women were kept mostly separate, and yet he had to confront a totally different set of circumstances when he moved out into the world. Unfortunately, rather than being able to integrate the male and female energies with honesty and integrity, he got lost in his attachments and ended up living a lie.

Conny has shared this remarkable anecdote with me:

*"It was 1973 in Seelisberg and I had been working with compiling a register of all the teachers of TM in the world at that time. Johnny Gray (author of "Men are from Mars, Women are from Venus") was then Skin Boy and came and got me for a private talk with Maharishi. Maharishi was pleased with the work I had been doing and said that he had a special task for me but that I was not to tell anyone outside of the inner circle about it. He wanted me to talk with many of the young men who worked for him and encourage them to become celibate. (I was already a practicing celibate at the time but had not taken vows.) We would call it the M group...M for monastery. If they, after some time felt comfortable with this lifestyle, then the plan was that they would take formal vows of celibacy. He said that he wanted to be surrounded by purity and that these young men would set an example for the others. So I threw myself into this new capacity and asked Clifford MacGuire to assist in the hunt."*

What *was* this? Did Maharishi feel so guilty that he projected his feelings onto others in the hopes that they would succeed where he had failed? Did he hope that their "purity" would give him strength where he was weak? Or was it all just part of a masterful cover up? After the first edition of this book was released, someone wrote to me and said that they once heard Maharishi say, "What this movement needs is a few good celibates!" That makes me think that he truly did believe that maintaining celibacy established a particular kind of spirituality that was worth being pursued. He just didn't feel *he* needed to pursue it.

Some of you who are reading this book may still consider yourselves to be devoted followers but after hearing my story feel tremendously disappointed when Maharishi no longer measures up to your idea of how a guru should be. For my part, I now realize that when I was that young woman in India, I needed to build Maharishi up as a fault free super being to bridge the gap of separation that existed within me. It was as if I had to make him a god to help convince myself that God really exists. Had I been able to experience the divinity within my *own* being to a larger degree, I wouldn't have needed to make *him* so divine.

Today I no longer believe in "perfect" human beings. We all have our strengths and weaknesses, even gurus. As long as one's feet walk the earth in the form of a human body, there is the possibility and probability of error.

# Was Maharishi an Enlightened Master?

The state of enlightenment is a favorite topic of discussion within many spiritual circles. Is this or that Master enlightened, was this or that master enlightened, Buddha became enlightened under that tree, that person just became enlightened, an enlightened brain functions this way or that way, etc., etc.

All this discussion makes me feel that the human race still has a way to go before we truly understand what the word enlightenment actually means. I have noticed that many people seem to equate the state of enlightenment with perfect wisdom and perfect ethics—if someone is enlightened they have the answers to all questions, and always act in a balanced and mature way.

For several decades I've been trying to get my head around Maharishi's obvious spiritual power and wisdom on the one hand, and his money/women attachments on the other. How can two or three seemingly totally opposing qualities make their home in the same body? But wait, doesn't that have to do with personality? And does personality actually affect how conscious we are or is personality just a collection of conditioned responses? I remember sometime during the 90's I started to think that enlightenment might just be a biological condition that doesn't necessarily have anything to do with how somebody acts or doesn't act. Mostly everyone I discussed this with did not agree... but I think that we should not confuse a certain code of ethics with a neurophysiological state of consciousness. Maybe enlightenment just has to do with how that person experiences reality. And maybe all of these intellectual definitions of enlightenment can be used as another mind trip by our egos to hang things up on.

So I guess the answer to whether or not Maharishi was an enlightened master will depend on your definition of enlightenment. To me he was not either-or; he was both. He was divine and he was human, just like all of us.

But in fulfilling his higher purpose, he was not just like all of us.

As the medium pointed out, Maharishi was in love with knowledge. So many memories I have are of sitting with him in a small group of devotees. We just sat there quietly, giving him the freedom to think and talk about the Vedic scriptures, one of his favorite pas-

All the four Vedas
sing the glory of
Creative Intelligence.
The original text books of
S.C.I. are the Vedas —

During
a moment of
inspiration, Maharishi has
written down a thought
that excites him.

times. He could get so excited about an insight in relation to some aspect of the Vedas.

I saved a piece of paper where he wrote this down after one of those moments:

*"All the four Vedas sing the glory of Creative Intelligence. The original text books of the Science of Creative Intelligence are the 4 Vedas."*

He loved the connection that he could see between the knowledge contained in the Vedas and various laws of physics (Maharishi had a college degree in physics). You can feel the joy and excitement in the way he wrote what is on this paper. First one color, and then he takes up another pen to write in another color, just for the fun of it.

Another note I saved contains a list of his intentions in the world:

• We shall make records.

- Write a book on practical philosophy of life
- Build Academies all over the world and
- Teach Transcendental Meditation to put an end to suffering and create a world of happiness and harmony.

*We are convinced the result of our efforts will be enjoyed by generations to come.*

These are the notes of a man who was joyfully consumed by his purpose. Maharishi achieved almost ev-

Maharishi's
handwritten
list of
personal
goals.

erything on his list. He revived interest for the knowledge in the Vedic scriptures, he wrote many books, he built meditation academies all over the world, and taught, indirectly through the teachers he trained, six million people to meditate. The world is not yet a place of happiness and harmony, but at least six million of us have a method for getting in touch with happiness and harmony on a regular basis if we allow ourselves to set aside time for meditating.

So as a celibate monk, denying his intimate contact with women or refusing ownership of material possessions, he was a failure. He went too far in his relationship to the West in terms of using our trust and our money.

But in the role of a seer with a true passion for knowledge and as a world changing personality with the desire to spread meditation throughout the world, I will defend him. In relation to his own culture, Maharishi was a courageous rebel. Meditation was not only for the initiated few…it was for the world.

To that rebel, enlightened or not, I am very thankful…had he not been so obsessed by the thought of spreading meditation, that little ad would not have jumped out at me from a Boston newspaper in 1968, announcing the lecture on Transcendental Meditation. He became my first spiritual teacher, showing me that my consciousness could change. And then he taught me how to teach others to experience that too.

Maharishi lecturing at Falsterbohus in Malmö, Sweden 1967.

Enjoy

Maharishi did what he loved to do. His favorite signature was "Enjoy". And we, his devotees, gave him the freedom to do that; by giving our love, our money, our energy, and our time.

# The Dharma[8] of Another Brings Danger

From the Bhagavad Gita, translation Maharishi Mahesh Yogi

Have you spent anytime reflecting on how many scandals we are surrounded by these days? Scandals involving presidents, popes, star athletes, banks, and even the Red Cross in Sweden, an institution I personally thought was beyond corruption. In June 2009 their Head of Communications was arrested for the embezzlement of large sums of money donated to the Red Cross.

Today I came across another piece. Channel 4 in England has broadcast on "Dispatches" that members of the Labour Party—and one Conservative—have sought highly paid work from an undercover TV re-

---

8  dharma: in this context: purpose, guiding principle, righteous duty.

porter pretending to be a lobbyist interested in hiring them. A former transport minister was secretly filmed offering to use his contacts for 5,000 pounds (currently $7,500) a day. In the footage he presents himself as someone who has been able to alter new laws "on behalf of" major companies.

And, interestingly, an institution I wrote about in the beginning of this book, the Catholic Church, is, as I am finishing it, almost daily in the news due to yet another scandal involving the sexual abuse of children during the 1970s by Catholic priests, this time in Germany.

So what's going on? Is the human race becoming more and more decadent? Or have human beings always been this dishonest and now we are just getting better at revealing it? I suppose the latter could be part of it...the media, through the use of the internet, has become exceedingly fast at spreading information worldwide. Yet from within all the spiritual circles I connect with I'm hearing a different message: it's more about the breakdown of the "old" ways of doing things. Soon we will be making evolutionary strides involving new attitudes, new values, new ways of exchanging goods and services, new ways of relating to each other and to the planet; in the meantime we are going through a cleansing process that is ridding our world of outmoded patriarchal systems. I hope this is true, because it is infinitely more positive than the way we are currently functioning. I don't believe that the human race will be able to sustain itself much longer on the basis of poor leadership.

One of Maharishi's weaknesses as a spiritual leader was to not encourage the qualities of true leadership within his teachers. He was so afraid that the steps he had taken to spread meditation throughout the world would be lost, that he focused more on his teachers as a source of distribution through the rote learning of procedures and practices, rather than encouraging devotees to be creative and think on their own. During the time I was with him I could see how he filtered out, with few exceptions, independent personalities, wishing to surround himself only with people who agreed with his way of doing things.

Ever since our conversation in the night revealing his desire to become Prime Minister of India, I have viewed Maharishi as a frustrated politician. When I heard, as the years passed, that he had built up a group of wealthy men he called rajas (monarchs) who were responsible for "governing" different areas in the world and had them dress in white robes with gold crowns, I realized he had simply created the world he wanted for himself, using funds donated to the organization. He was a genius at creating and recreating himself as a messiah for thousands of spiritually inclined people who longed to find one.

So now that Maharishi is gone, my guess is that there is plenty of chaos at the top of the TM pyramid, since no one has really been trained to think or act on their own and the conditions for wanting to elbow each other out have been in place all along. And I wish that Maharishi had not set a precedent of making such exaggerated claims coupled with high fees, since that only sets people up for disappointment further down the road. The tragic thing is that the meditation technique itself is good enough to stand on its own, yet the incongruities within the marketing strategies of the movement that create confusion and distrust persist. Is the TM movement about teaching a simple and effective method to relax and refresh yourself, or is it about learning how to "levitate" and become "invisible?" by joining evermore demanding courses?

But even though we seem to be taking out the garbage from formerly relied upon organizations, systems and beliefs, I do think it is unrealistic to expect that we won't feel a need for spiritual leadership. Human beings get very confused in changing times, and the kind of change we are currently experiencing is of a different caliber. My grandchildren are going to have to grow up with the realization that our present daily regimes are actually knocking out life supporting eco systems on earth. When I was a child, the earth seemed hugely untouchable. Now I feel a collective urgency. There is a shared awareness that we have damaged the planet without being sure that we know what to do about it. Where should we turn? What kind of leadership do we need to be able to keep on living on our pretty blue planet?

There is a wonderful word that we have started using in a new way: sustainable. 50 years ago that word would most likely have been used in reference to whether or not the floor we were walking on would hold our own weight. Probably due to what's happening in the environment we are now using it with regard to technology, agricultural methods, city planning, etc. So how about "sustainable leadership"?

What would that be for me? Especially with regard to the harm that can be caused by exaggerated involvement with a controlling religious sect (or any large company, political party and organization for that matter), it would have to include a greater sense of trust in oneself. I can only be an expert on the time in the world that I have experienced and within my own sphere, but what I see is that no one I know from my generation and culture, has truly been encouraged since childhood to rely on their own thinking. This may be especially true for women. I have no memory of anyone ever asking me as a young person, "What do you think about this situation?" I was taught that everyone else was an authority except myself...my parents, my school teachers, the church, the news on television, and later on anyone with a doctor's degree.

So perhaps the most important preparation for sustainable leadership would be for all of us who habitually seek wisdom outside of ourselves to put more time and effort into bringing our own male and female energies, our own logic and intuition, into enough balance to give birth to our own divine knowingness. This is a process that can take a whole lifetime (it has and is for me), but if I compare what was available when I was growing up to what is available now in terms of methodologies, tools and teachings, there is no real reason why this kind of awakening cannot move so much faster. Thankfully, many of the children being raised today are being brought up by parents who are allowing their children to maintain a stronger sense of themselves.

More than ever we need our spiritual leaders to inspire us by being living examples of what they represent, to walk their talks. But it's equally important that the rest of us are willing to share responsibility with our leaders. The part of us that is an all too willing devotee can also be the part of us that seeks a comfort zone of avoiding having to think on our own. If we are going to criticize the way Maharishi ran his movement, we also have to be willing to look at our own eagerness to follow.

Other qualities of sustainable leadership could include feedback systems, responsibility rotation, and including children in our decision making processes... they, for sure, will be thinking further than the next election, particularly with regard to what's going on with an environment which may or may not be able to support them when they have become adults. And if there are any young people reading this book, I would say, do not let a spiritual teacher decide for you whether or not you should lead a life of heterosexuality, homosexuality or celibacy. The kundalini energy or sexual force is a powerful force that the human race really needs to learn a lot more about, but following the advice of teachers who preach one thing and live another just adds to the confusion.

There is a verse in the Bhagavad Gita[9], translated by

9  The Bhagavad Gita (meaning "Song of God") is a sacred Hindu text consisting of 700 verses describing a dialogue between Arjuna and Lord Krishna on the battlefield. It is often referred to as a guide for how to live one's life.

Maharishi: *Better is death in one's own dharma (purpose, duty, guiding principle): the dharma of another brings danger.*

His interpretation of the translation includes the following: "It is evident from this that there is a yet greater danger to life than the phenomenon of death. A greater danger will be something that actually retards the process of evolution. The dharma of another belongs to a level of evolution different from one's own. Because man has freedom of action, ... he is capable of attempting to perform actions suitable to the dharma of another. But if he performs such actions, he loses the continuity of progress on the level from which he could evolve. This is the greatest danger to life: that one lives life, time goes by, without any progress on the path of evolution." In other words, instead of asking our gurus, our messiahs, our heroes, what to do when we feel uncertain, maybe we should start by asking ourselves one question: *am I living my purpose or someone else's?*

It's interesting...books and films often start and finish in the form of a circle. The circle of this book is bringing me back to what I said to the priest when I was 16...that I believed we should try to decide for ourselves what's right and wrong and then do our best to live by that. I have forgotten that many, many times in my life, when I allowed someone I viewed wiser than myself to influence my decisions.

# Maharishi's Mantras

There is a lot of debate outside the TM movement with regard to the Vedic mantras Maharishi selected.

For Hindus, the mantras cause no concern. They are part and parcel of the ancient holy scriptures (perhaps 4000 years old) that their faith regards as an authority. Yet these mantras, their meaning or lack of it, how they are chosen, and their traditional use is a clouded subject for students of TM and an area that creates a lot of conflict for orthodox practitioners of other faiths. A summation of Maharishi's comments on this subject could read, "The mantra has a specific effect, but since we only use it on a sound level and not a meaning level, you don't need to bother about what the meaning is."

Water pattern    Sand pattern

Sand pattern    Water pattern

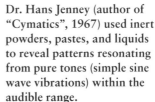

Dr. Hans Jenney (author of "Cymatics", 1967) used inert powders, pastes, and liquids to reveal patterns resonating from pure tones (simple sine wave vibrations) within the audible range.

If the meaning is of no consequence, why have different mantras at all?

Personally, if I am going to repeat a word over and over again, at deeper levels of my psyche, year in and year out, I want to know what it means or stands for and I can understand the criticism that has been directed toward the TM movement on this point. Some of the mantras are Bija (seed) mantras (stem sounds without meaning), but not all.

But to go so far as to suggest that it does not matter what mantra one uses, which is the way many allopathically trained advocates of meditation have chosen to go, is an even bigger mistake.

After all, "In the beginning was the word, and the word was with God."

The idea that the resonance of a particular mantra, or sound, creates a specific manifestation effect is fascinating. Instead of insisting that the meaning of a mantra is of no particular consequence, why not go in the opposite direction? Let's discuss this issue more openly and do more research on the mantras and their effects?

Many people ask me about my current stance with regard to practicing TM. I still practice and teach meditation as Maharishi taught me, including performing the puja, but use a different set of Vedic mantras, one for each chakra. I love meditating and find that it refreshes me and keeps me connected with what I define as a spiritual path. *If* my clients want to know the meaning of their mantra I will tell them, but advise them not to put any focus on that meaning during meditation. If performing a puja creates a conflict for them, I do not perform it but give thanks within. If there is any problem with the mantra for a person with an orthodox Christian, Muslim, or Jewish background, we talk it through and select another mantra that does not collide with their belief systems. I do not promise my clients enlightenment, and I don't charge 2300 Euro for four one hour lessons in meditation.

Maharishi's notes on a Sanskrit mantra from the Rig Veda with regard to the distribution of wealth.

Maharishi would often scribble notes during meetings and then leave them behind. If he wanted something preserved he would instead ask someone to take dictation. These notes are from interviews with his prospective teachers who have come from many different countries and raised problems concerning the mantras they were using with respect to their language of origin.

# A Message to My Sisters

By "my sisters" I mean, in this case, all of the other women who had intimate contact with Maharishi Mahesh Yogi. To my knowledge, I am the first to come out in front of a film camera and say, yes, the rumors are true...and I was one of the women involved. So now that's done.

I invite you to get in touch with me if you want to have someone to talk to about your experience. (My email address and telephone number are easy to find on my websites.) I swear that that conversation will remain confidential and also want you to know that I have no judgments about whether the experience was heaven or hell for you. Obviously, I will believe your story.

If you would prefer to keep your secret, I understand why. There are so many reasons, aren't there? You might be thinking of how this news would affect your current relationship or family members. You might be thinking of how it would affect your career, since you may still be involved with the TM community or have Maharishi as a part of your marketing image. You may feel you will cause harm or worry about embarrassment. You might just still be afraid, period. Whatever your reason, I understand because I have carried many of these reasons within me for all these years.

But I can also say how telling the truth about my relationship with this man has been such a tremendous relief on so many levels, and that I am absolutely sure it is the right thing to do, at least for me. It was time to let go of the denial; it is time.

If you have read the whole book, you know by now that I am no longer worried about causing Maharishi any harm...in fact I believe I am helping him to freedom as he is off in some loka (dimension) preparing for his next lifetime. The energy surrounding this entire project has been overwhelmingly positive.

And as for Mia Farrow's world famous association with Maharishi, well, so many statements have been made by other people who appear to be authorities on *her* experience, but as far as I know, they were not in the same room that Maharishi and Mia were in.

There is only one person we should listen to regarding that matter...and that is Mia herself. She writes about it in her 1997 autobiography "What Falls Away."

Please, feel free to write or call.

# It is Done,
# It is Done,
# It is Done

NASA started to beam the Beatles song "Across the Universe" at 0000 hours GMT on February 5, 2008 to celebrate their 45th anniversary of the day NASA's deep-space communications network was set up. A few hours later on the same day, Maharishi Mahesh Yogi left his body. The music was beamed on a 431 light-year journey to the North Star, Polaris, where it should arrive year 2439. John Lennon wrote this song during the time the Beatles were learning Transcendental Meditation from Maharishi, which explains the salutation "Jai Guru Deva" in the chorus line.

Journalists called it "cosmic coincidence," "too weird for fiction," and "cosmic fluke." As a practitioner of Shamanic healing rites, I see it differently. My intuitive feeling about Maharishi's last years is that he could have left a couple of years earlier. In a sense, he may have been "kept here" by the human needs of thousands of devotees who simply did not want him to leave, and perhaps even family members who also may have had their own reasons for not letting him go. I did not feel a lot of emotion when he died, having let go of him many, many years ago.

Sometimes the wishes and needs of humans make it difficult for a soul to leave the body to continue on its path into other dimensions. So I don't see the timing of the Beatles song being projected into space with

Maharishi's death as an unexplainable coincidence. I think the energy in the song, Jai Guru Deva Om, directed at a distant star, was the perfect help the master needed to be able to leave the planet. Or else, he just wanted to leave with style. He always did have a flair for the dramatic.

What can I say? There was a great power in you Maharishi and in your higher purpose.

I am still in awe that our paths were intertwined for a time here on Earth.

You asked me if I was going to keep you in the dark. This book is my answer.

I sincerely hope it follows you all the way into the light as you journey across the universe.

# Afterword and Witness Testimonial

*The Statement of a Witness*

Allow me to introduce Dr. Robert McCutchan, also a former teacher of Transcendental Meditation. Rob and I were in India together, and as fate would have it, the title of this book came through him. He had originally planned to use it himself, but in the end he let go of the project and when I contacted him for the first time in decades, he generously allowed me to use it. The following is a brief description of his personal history with the TM movement, as well as what he observed about the relationship between Maharishi and me in Rishikesh. We never spoke with each other on this subject during that time period, and I never realized that he had seen so much, until a few years ago:

*"In the fall of 1967 I was initiated into the practice of Transcendental Meditation by Jerry Jarvis (then head of the Students' International Meditation Society) in Berkeley, California. After meditating for a few months, I had a classic experience of the awakening*

**Maharishi in Kashmir 1968.**

*of Kundalini, and the ecstatic bliss of this convinced me of the profound value of meditation. I decided to become more involved in the TM movement.*

*After attending a subsequent month-long course conducted by Maharishi in Squaw Valley during the summer of 1968, I returned to my studies at the University of Colorado and started a TM center at the Boulder campus. This center quickly grew into one of the largest and most active in America. As a result of this success, I was accepted to attend the fall 1969 Teachers' Training course in Rishikesh, India.*

*During that course, I had even more powerful experiences of awakening Kundalini which produced not only inner bliss, but also the external experience of what was then called in the movement God Consciousness—the actual visual appearance of divinely radiant golden light suffusing all of relative existence. After the second of the experiences mentioned above, I recounted it at one of the evening lectures when we were encouraged to share the results of our practice. Maharishi responded by saying, "Beautiful, beautiful!" over and over again. At the end of the lecture, he stroked my head and called me his "Golden Boy." I then became one of his favorites, and he began greeting me personally and asking how I was doing.*

*Later on Maharishi asked me if it would be possible for me to stay on for the next Teachers' Training course which was to begin in January of 1970. He wanted me to help with the new trainees and with other tasks at the Ashram. I eagerly accepted and became, along with Abhay, one of Maharishi's "Skin Boys"—a* name derived from one of our duties, which was to carry his deerskin and place it wherever he was going to sit. Abhay and I became fast friends, and shared the joy of being so close to the Master and carrying out whatever tasks he assigned us.

Not long after the new trainees arrived, Maharishi began showing a lot of interest in a young American girl named Judith Bourque. I remember her reading a poem she had written at a lecture and afterwards he asked if she would to come to his house occasionally and read poetry to him in the evenings. She naturally was enthused by this attention from the Master and eagerly agreed. Soon after, MMY sent me and Abhay to Judith's room late one night to get her and escort her back to his villa. We did this five or six times, and then evidently Judith and MMY began making arrangements on their own for her to continue her visits clandestinely.

These visits were, however, not unnoticed by me and Abhay. Sometimes after Maharishi had told us to "go and rest," instead of going to bed we would sit in a nook on the veranda of his house, wrapped in blankets and talk quietly of our hopes and dreams. Our voices were masked by the roar of the Ganges River down the cliffs from the Ashram, and we were in a secluded spot where we could not readily be seen. From this vantage point we would occasionally notice Judith coming down the path to Maharishi's house late at night after everyone else had retired for the evening.

At first, we didn't make much of these furtive, nocturnal visits, but over time we began to joke about the "poetry girl," and the real purpose of her late-night comings and goings. While a deeply buried part of me suspected the truth, that they were in fact lovers, the "true believer" in me could not admit what seemed to be going on. Abhay, however, who actually lived in a room in Maharishi's house, must have seen or heard something that I didn't, because I began to notice a distinct change in his attitude and appearance. When we first became friends, our talks were of our devotion to Maharishi and our desire to serve the Master. Gradually, Abhay became more and more negative about and even contemptuous of Maharishi, and instead of talking about his desire to serve, he began to talk about wanting to emigrate to the United States and to take up a new life there. He also began neglecting his appearance, and seemed ever more lost and disconsolate. In retrospect I now believe that he had some sort of direct knowledge that Maharishi and Judith were lovers, and it was this discovery that led to his increasing disaffection. At the time, we never discussed this specifically, and in my naivety I continued to serve Maharishi until the end of the second Teachers' Training course, and then left the Ashram to travel back to the U.S.

I returned to Boulder in the fall of 1970 where I had a final semester of classes to complete my undergraduate requirements. Maharishi decided to hold his next Teachers' Training course in the United States, and as it turned out, this course was held in Estes Park, Colorado, just a pleasant drive away from Boulder. I ended up suggesting and then arranging a tremendously successful lecture held by Maharishi on the university campus. The largest lecture hall on campus was packed, and there were many members of the print and television media there. This was sort of the grand culmination of all of the work I had done to make the Boulder TM center flourish, and I was very proud and happy that it all went so well. After the lecture, as we were walking to his car, Maharishi said to me that I should get much of the credit for the success of TM in Colorado and that he would like to have me join his international staff. I was overjoyed at this opportunity, and within days was winging my way to the Spanish island of Mallorca where the next Teachers' Training courses were to be held.

I stayed with Maharishi for the duration of five years during which I became his first Western Brahmachari (celibate monk). The last time I saw Judith was in Mallorca. After that, she left the movement and never came back. It was also in Mallorca that I witnessed the same pattern of late night visits with Belinda, a pretty, blond, brown-eyed young girl from Oregon. Sarees were arranged for her, as well as an excuse to meet... this time it was going through the mail. Once again I was sent to fetch a young woman and was left to wait outside the Master's door. When Belinda finally emerged, she came out looking rumpled and mussed.

My mind then went back to India and Judith's visits to read Maharishi poetry, and I again had an intuition about what was going on, but my "true believer" mentality would not permit me to deduce what otherwise would have seemed obvious. Belinda apparently had a change of heart during her stay in Mallorca and abruptly left, and I saw Maharishi regress into an emotional state reminiscent of a lovesick, bewildered teenager. At the time, none of us knew why she had left. Much later, through a mutual friend of Belinda's and mine, I learned that she had left because she had become Maharishi's lover and that the whole business so confused, depressed, and upset her that she decided she had to get out.

That I had been there for both of these assignations made the friend's story instantly credible. It finally became obvious that Maharishi was urging us to be celibate at the same time as he was breaking his own vows. This scenario and the unfolding of subsequent events led me in time to break with Maharishi, concluding three of the most eventful and joyful years of my life. I left the TM movement and fortunately was able to find other ways to continue on my spiri-

tual path. I am proud of Judith for finally coming forward with the truth, and exorcising these debilitating ghosts from the past. May her story keep others from replicating it, should they find themselves in similar circumstances."


*Rob McCutchan*

223

# Four Years
## Later...

**To:** judithbourque@email.com
**Subject:** Greetings from Fairfield! I loved your book

Dear Judith,

I just finished reading your book and couldn't put it down. Thank you for writing i
It took a lot of courage to do what you did" and you did the right thing. I've been
and the first 7 or 8 years I thought Maharishi was a perfect person who couldn't m
happened that woke me up to the fact that he was definitely wrong about a few th
man with a big dream and a lot of energy to fulfill his dream.

Anyway, I have sooooooo many things I want to say to you, but I will keep it dow

1) I believe that you are telling the truth.

---

**B** *I* <u>U</u> | More ≋ | ☺ | Stationery

**To:** judithbourque@email.com
**Subject:** RE: your book

Dear Judith,

Thank you again for your beautifull book, which I read for the second
enjoyed his life for 200%, that means at least also the relative for 10
whole truth about his being a monk, which he apparently was not full
the great master I thought he was, but still he was a great teacher ar
very much what he taught me.

---

**B** *I* <u>U</u> | More ≋ | ☺ | Stationery

**To:** judithbourque@email.com
**Subject:** Robes of Silk

Hi Judith,

I just finished reading your book. I want to thank you for having the
courage to publish it and expose yourself in such a vulnerable way.
You did a great job of expressing such a delicate situation and how it
impacted your life and heart. And I am glad that you were able to
continue your spiritual journey through other forms and explorations.
Maharishi was responsible for starting us all out on our path back
then and giving us a very strong foundation in meditation. I will
always be greatful for that and for the 10 years I had with MMY.

# In the Mail

Oddly enough, I didn't think much about what the reaction to my book would be as I was writing it. I just knew it was time to pull the cork. Imagine my surprise when emails started pouring in, filled with gratitude and appreciation! What follows are a few anonymous (and some not anonymous) excerpts:

*"I just finished reading your book and couldn't put it down. Thank you for writing it. You can't be told this enough: 'It took a lot of courage to do what you did' and you did the right thing. I've been a TM meditator for over 30 years, and the first 7 or 8 years I thought Maharishi was a perfect person who couldn't make*

*mistakes. Then something happened that woke me up to the fact that he was definitely wrong about a few things. Now I simply see him as a man with a big dream and a lot of energy to fulfill his dream."*

*"I just finished reading your book. I want to thank you for having the courage to publish it and expose yourself in such a vulnerable way. You did a great job of expressing such a delicate situation and how it impacted your life and heart. Maharishi was responsible for starting us all out on our path back then and (for) giving us a very strong foundation in meditation. I will always be grateful for that and for the ten years I had with MMY. I had heard about your book when it first came out but thought I didn't want to read it thinking it would be too disturbing. I had heard the talk about Maharishi and women from friends, but it was never really confirmed until now. It is very obvious that your story is not fabricated. But I didn't find it disturbing at all. It's hard when someone who impacted your life so deeply and whom I held with such respect represents themselves in a false way. And though I feel that MMY's relations with money and power lacked integrity from my stand point, I still have great compassion for the inner struggles he must have battled with."*

*"Thank you again for your beautiful book, which I read for the second time. I am sure now that Maharishi really enjoyed his life 200%! It is only a pity that he didn't tell us the whole truth about his being a monk, which he apparently was not full time. Your book*

*made me clear that he was not the great master I thought he was, but still he was a great teacher and I loved him very much and still appreciate very much what he taught me."*

*"Yesterday I finished reading your book and since then have not been able to stop thinking about it. Another TM teacher loaned the book to me and in the beginning I really didn't want to read it. I had pre-conceptions about your reasons for writing the book and perhaps even hoped that those thoughts would be proven when I read it. But instead I feel great trust in everything you related and feel very grateful to you for sharing your experiences."*

*"Reading your book, Judith, was a physical experi-ence: I felt tensions in my body and heart releasing. I never expected this to happen. Amazing—and I am sure this effect goes well beyond anything you intended. But I felt like I was in a room alone with Maharishi, with him reminding me of the powerful in-fluence he still has over me. Whew. I feel everyone who knew, who came close to, who counted Maharishi as their beloved Master, must read this book."*

*"I am reading your book at night before I go to bed —it's wonderful. It's honest and interesting. It's so much about our way into a world that has no script other than the prescription script that doesn't fit. It's the story of so many young women, even though it is about extraordinary events and people."*

*"Judith, I have finished your book and I'm searching for something to say in appreciation of it that you haven't already heard. I'm failing. I am so impressed with your candor, your objectivity, and your generosity—towards yourself, towards M, towards your entire experience. Since I left TMO in 197X I have been asked to write or to help write "exposes" of M and the movement by disgruntled former teachers. I have always refused on the grounds that such an act is more often motivated by vengeance than by altruism or true responsibility. But your book is kind, and intelligent, and says what needs to be said. It is a compelling and very human story.*

*I hope it is widely read, and if properly understood, will go towards helping all of us humans to see through our false understandings of Teachers and their roles in our lives. It may even help some Teachers see through their false understanding of our role in their lives!"*

*"Reading your book has had some very subtle liberating effect on me. Not dismissing "the knowledge" but recognizing the very human element of MMY that makes him even more endearing to me. It was like an advanced technique! I don't like... that he deceived all of us and the possible psychological harm he created in some women he had affairs with. That was just plain irresponsible and unethical on his part. He should have done better. But I'll always value MMY for the understanding of the transcendent dimension he brought to my life and, more importantly, the transcendent experience his techniques and presence allowed."*

– Peter L. Sutphen

*"I found your book deeply moving. I didn't expect such an emotional response to the story of your relationship with Maharishi since I had little contact with him during my years in the TM movement. I guess that the degree of my response demonstrates the powerful effect of gurus and religious movements on young followers. If my peripheral involvement left such a deep impression, I can only imagine what it must be like for you and other members of the inner circle. Perhaps your greatest achievement is to reveal Maharishi's human side. So many people think of him as super-human—a divine savior or an evil super villain. You reveal him as an ordinary man doing all the good and bad things that love and sex can inspire in us. I never felt any sort of human connection with him until I read your book. Maybe your story is so moving because, on one level, it's a universal tale of love and loss. We've all been to the giddy heights and awful depths of love. Any reader can recognize their own feelings in your book and use that experience as a path into the unique and deeply strange world of Maharishi's movement. You have given the world a great gift."*

*– Geoff Gilpin, author "The Maharishi Effect*


*"Some people tell me that your book is just gossip and negativity and that they don't see the point of it. To that I usually reply that gossip is the spreading of questionable second-hand information in order to shock and upset and entertain malice. This book is something else, completely. It's a witness statement, and a*

231

*positive one, since it brings out the human perspective and leaves space for acceptance and forgiveness and truth. It is a comfort and vindication for the abused and rejected. It is the spirituality of the new age, since it is based on transparency instead of hierarchy."*

*— Anders Rosenberg, Media Creator*

What also poured in were your stories. What I mean is that you shared what had happened to you in your experiences with Maharishi and his TM movement. One of my readers wrote, "I wish I had a TM Anonymous group to go to." Many who wrote were ex-TM teachers and had been part of the movement for anywhere from 8 to 15 to 30 years...some were still active as teachers of Transcendental Meditation.

*"Even if your love affair with Maharishi is probably felt to be the most spectacular in the book, I am very happy that you were critical about his strange relationship to money."*

*"I attended many TTC and ATR courses throughout the seventies. I was very disillusioned with MMY over the TM movement's relationship to money and power - which both saddened me and confused me."*

*"It takes 10 minutes to learn TM and a lifetime to sort through all the inconsistencies and lies along with all the wonderful blessings and benefits. E-gads!"*

*"Looking back at that (experience) and other clues I*

*had picked up here and there, I realized that there was a certain level of sexual impropriety that was/is tolerated in the Transcendental Meditation Organization. It's secret, and you only catch a glimpse of it if you're 'in the know.' On the one hand, they seem very chaste. Sex isn't talked about, or if it is, people are very embarrassed and want to move on from THAT conversation. And yet the sex is there, and it is happening— sometimes in odd and inappropriate ways."*

*"I have been deeply involved in the TM-movement up until 1991, including five years on Purusha. I hardly need to say that there were (and probably still are) no realistic teachings on emotions and sexuality in this movement, apart from some other 'disasters' I encountered there also. Your book was a good and fine read for me. Actually, I was a little surprised I could read it so well with so much calmness of mind. I passed the book on to a lady TM-teacher I had first met in 197x, when I was on TM-staff in 19XX. She was very happy to receive it, and now the book and knowledge will start circulating more and more in the TM-movement in my country I expect. It will have some good influence on sexual morals and other things in meditators' lives I hope. Thanks very much for coming out so boldly and being so greatly polite at the same time."*

And here is a funny one from Casey Coleman, one of the "Skin boys" who knew me:

*"I just read your book, Robes of Silk Feet of Clay and I loved it ! It brought back memories of a fun time in my life. And seeing the past from a different perspective brought both a sweet joy and insight into my "true believer" past. I liked the tone of the book, my MMY experience was totally positive and he was always very good to me. The first thing I experienced when learning that MMY had a secret life was amazement that he slept even less than I thought!"*

I've read and tried to answer all of your letters, but in case I missed someone, I just want to say thank you for the moral support you've shown by sending me your feedback. These letters showed me that "coming out" was, in fact, the right decision for me. Your letters have also led me to the following conclusion: that whenever a spiritual movement makes celibacy a general rule or higher principal to be followed by its members, even if the original intention is a "noble" one, trouble follows. It appears that denying our God-given creative force makes it only that much more fascinating for spiritual teachers, and that attempts to control devotees on this subject have often caused serious hurt and confusion.

Others have asked for more details regarding our love-making, curious in particular about whether or not Maharishi was into "spiritual sex" or something tantric. I can say this much: when we had our affair, he was like a teenager. In that sense, we were both young and inexperienced. My opinion is that he suffered from a gap in what we view as "normal" social development with regard to having a healthy, mutual, sexual relationship with a woman due to his years of prolonged celibacy as a Brahmachari at his Master's ashram. So no, there was no discussion or practice of anything one might want to label "spiritual" sex. For me it was simply having the opportunity to be that close to someone I loved very much.

Many of you have also called by phone, or we have chatted over Skype or even met if I have been in your area. The question everyone asks is whether or not I have been in contact with any other women who have had similar experiences with Maharishi. The answer to that is **yes**. To date I know of fourteen other women who had experiences with him (of varying degrees) that did not jibe with the role of a celibate monk. Several of these reports are from first hand dialog, the rest are second hand from a person who knew the woman in question very well such as a partner or close friend. In fact, it recently came to my knowledge that Maharishi has a daughter living in the United States. It is my understanding that an agreement is in place in order to protect the identity of her biological father. I find that sad. He should have been proud to have a daughter. Many have also said how great it would be if at least one other woman would come out and tell her story. At the time I wrote the first edition of this book such was not the case. However, recently I have been in touch with someone who has also made the decision to "come out". I will continue to protect the identities of the women who have been in touch with me until the day, if ever, they choose to share what happened to them.

# Returning to Rishikesh

Long, long ago, there was a battle in the heavens between the devas and the demons. They were fighting
over a vessel containing Amrit (ambrosia), the nectar
of immortality and salvation, each side wanting to have
its powers. Lord Vishnu finally tricked the demons by
transforming himself into the beautiful Mohini, who
made the demons forget all about the Amrit while he
was secretly distributing it to the devas. In the struggles
between the two sides, drops of the nectar were spilled
and fell to earth in four places in India: Haridwar,
Allahabad, Ujjain, and Nashik. These four places
alternately host the Kumbh Mela festival every three
years, with the larger Purna Kumbh Mela celebrated

every twelve years in the city of Allahabad. These festivals attract millions of pilgrims since their meaning is important for Hindus. The power of these geographical areas provides enough grace to wash away all their sins by bathing in the holy rivers located there.

What could be more appropriate than to take our eighth and as far as we knew final Master Class to at least one of these cities? And to Rishikesh, in the foothills of the Himalayas where it all started for us as young, hopeful teachers of Transcendental Meditation.

Since 2006, Conny and I had brought together a group of spiritually inclined people for the purpose of developing together. We weren't trying to start a new movement since we were laden with scars from experiences of having been too deeply involved in other movements. In a way, we started an *anti-movement*. So rather than have one method of evolving, we shared many methods and skills. Participants became teachers. The seminar was free with a low administrative cost. We kept it small...thirty to forty participants was the usual size. We maintained little or no contact with participants during the year and simply encouraged them to follow their own destinies within their chosen fields until we would meet again the following year. New ones came. Old ones passed through. We called it the Master Class because we were all becoming our own masters, our own gurus. Step by step each one of us was learning to find the confidence to hold his or her piece of the puzzle in the greater purpose of things.

Organizing the trip was nerve racking for me. We had a lot of ground to cover in eighteen days, and yet we wanted to do more than just sight-see. Some members had never been to India, and we wanted to take them to Varanasi, Bodhgaya, Sarnath, Delhi, Haridwar and finally Rishikesh. Still, the true significance of why we ended up traveling to where we traveled seemed to be revealed first after we arrived at each spot.

## Dying in Varanasi

We booked our flights so as to arrive on a full moon at Varanasi, the oldest and holiest city in all of India.

Early the next morning, as we walked down the long steps leading to the Ganges, it felt as though we stepped into an energy of love. This took me by surprise due to my conditioned mental associations with all the cremations that took place at this spot. But why not? This was a place where families and friends say prayers for the souls of their dear ones. On our boat ride we cruised past temples and burning funeral pyres and saw eagles flying high above our heads.

After the boat ride, our guide walked us through the town and pointed out some elders sitting in the midst of all the hustle and bustle of a busy city. He said, "You might think that those people you see are beggars, but they are not. They have come here to die." He went on to explain that Hindus believe they will reach moksha if they die in Varanasi, which means they will be freed from the cycle of death and rebirth known as reincarnation.

"This must be a good place to die," I thought. By constructing a small sculpture or talisman representing what we wanted to let go of, we could pass through a

Varanasi: Early the next morning, as we walked down the long steps leading to the Ganges, it felt as though we stepped into an energy of love.

Left: Varanasi: Boat ride on the Ganges at dawn.

Below: Funeral pyre.

symbolic death here in order to release that which no longer served us. This was a process I had learned from shamanic healing, the teaching being that negative energy cannot be destroyed, but it *can* be transformed. Later that night, everyone carried their small "compositions" complete with words such as ill health, grief, guilt, poverty, etc. along on our next boat ride on the Ganges. We lighted them with a match and released the old, no longer needed parts of ourselves into the cleansing waters of the holy mother. As our boat slowly cruised along the river, we were accompanied by chiming bells and swirling flames of burning ghee. Priests

Many elders come to Varanasi to spend the last part of their lives. They believe that by dying in Varanasi they will reach moksha.

Varanasi: Our moonlight ride on the Ganges River to the chimes and mantras of evening Aarti performed by seven priests.

sang the puja mantras for evening Aarti, a ceremony they perform every evening of every day of every year.

Maharishi had instructed all of his teachers of Transcendental Meditation to perform a puja ceremony when we taught someone to meditate, but this was a seven fold puja since seven priests were performing the rite at the same time. Our guide told us that this ceremony also contained prayers for the entire world, not just India. That impressed me. Seven priests praying simultaneously for the entire world every night... not just their own country.

## Bussing to Bodhgaya

The trip continued on to Sarnath, where Buddha first began to teach, and then to Bodhgaya where he became enlightened. The 6 hour bus ride to Bodhgaya had worried me tremendously while organizing the trip. We would only

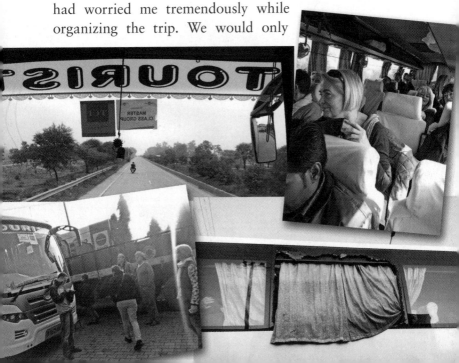

have one night in Bodhgaya itself and that meant six hours there and six hours back of sitting on a bus driving over bumpy roads with poor access to toilets. Would our group handle it?

Not only did they handle it...they turned it into a vision quest with a superb attitude, even when the window of our bus accidently got knocked out by the driver. These lovely pilgrims used the time to talk and get to know each other better, or rest and meditate.

Finally there, as we walked through the entrance to this

A leaf from the Bohdi tree at Bodhgaya.

World Heritage Monument, a wave of positive energy washed over me, almost as though someone had thrown a bucket of warm water at me. We spent several hours there, walking in Buddha's footsteps, tasting the energy of enlightenment as we moved through the different areas where Buddha had meditated after he had become awakened. Many of the areas of the

Behind the wall covered with garlands of flowers is the very spot where it is said that Buddha became enlightened.

temple were crowded with visitors and munks, but wherever we stood, sat or meditated the atmosphere was thick with stillness and tranquility. It was worth the long ride in the bus!

Haridwar: We met with a pundit whose special role was to assist with prayers for those family members who had passed on.

This is Har ki Pauri ghat at Haridwar where, according to legend, drops of amrit fell to the earth.

## Pundits in Haridwar

In the ancient city of Haridwar, we put our feet into the Ganges River at Har ki Pauri ghat (Har ki Pauri = footsteps of the lord, in this case Lord Vishnu). This is the most famous spot of the city, the place for ritualistic bathing to wash away sins and attain enlightenment. We also said prayers for our family members who had passed on as is the custom at this particular spot on the Ganges River, where the drops of immortality fell from the heavens.

247

## Hanuman welcomes us to Rishikesh

The climax of our trip was Rishikesh, where we slowed our pace down and started the remainder of our Master Class process. Just a year earlier, the Ganges had suddenly swelled to cause vicious flooding and landslides that had affected the lives of tens of thousands in the area and was now labeled as a "Himalayan Tsunami". A huge statue of Shiva constructed on the riverbanks of the Ganges here had finally been swept away by the flood. This would be the third Tsunami affected area my feet had touched upon within a time period of ten years.

Once settled at our hotel we shifted into a daily routine of long group meditations, shamanic healing and messages, ceremonies, experience sharing, and excur-

This very large statue of Lord Hanuman is located in downtown Rishikesh. Hanuman is a Hindu Diety known for his courage, power and selfless service. In the epic story of Rama and Sita (the dieties of the perfect man and perfect woman) he is central to the return of Sita who has been captured by Ravana, the demon king. At one point in the epic, his devotion is questioned, whereupon he tears open his heart to reveal that yes, both Rama and Sita are there; his love is pure.

sions to various points of history and power embedded in the foothills of the Himalayas.

And, of course, a visit to Maharishi's old ashram was a must. After all, Conny and I both had powerful memories connected to the ashram. For me it had been an unusual and incredible love affair, a relationship that would set the course for the rest of my life in many ways. Conny also became a teacher of TM there and prepared the ground to later become one of Maharishi's "skin boys". But perhaps of even deeper meaning for him were the three full days he got to spend with the then most famous saint of the area, Tat Wale Baba. After nagging Maharishi for weeks, he had finally been given permission to go and spend time

Maharishi sitting with visiting Pundits at his Rishikesh ashram during our Teacher Training program. I am standing in the background with three other devotees.

© Jonathan Miller

Above: Rishikesh: View up toward the Himalayan foothills.

Below: The steps by the Ganges where the Aarti ceremony was performed in Rishikesh every evening. Only the base of the giant statue of Shiva remains after it was consumed by floods in 2013.

My turn to carry the flame during the evening puja.

with the renowned saint by his cave, even "earning" a cave of his own to come back to whenever he wished, said Tat Wale Baba. Maharishi was very eager to interview Conny when he got back from the visit, and listened with intense interest as Conny described all of the extraordinary things he had experienced. He had seen Tat Wale Baba actually levitate, and this wasn't a matter of hopping like a frog. He had simply risen from the ground in luminous stillness. Conny says Maharishi acted as though it was confirmation of a rumor

A part of our Rishikesh pilgrimage was total emersion in Mother Ganges. It was cold and clean up here in the mountains!

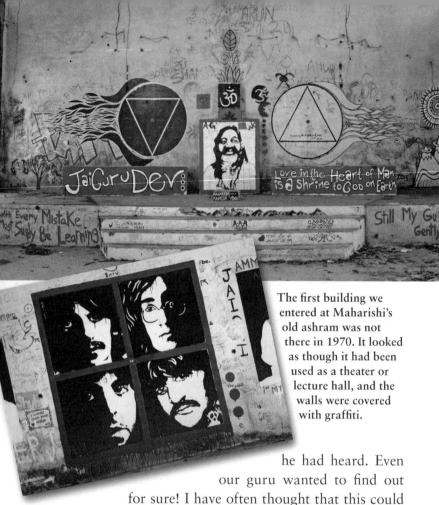

The first building we entered at Maharishi's old ashram was not there in 1970. It looked as though it had been used as a theater or lecture hall, and the walls were covered with graffiti.

he had heard. Even our guru wanted to find out for sure! I have often thought that this could have been the seed of his later fascination with developing supernatural powers through the TM-Sidhi program. So our quest became both to visit the old TM ashram and to find what remained of Tat Wale Baba's caves as well.

The walk to Maharishi's ashram was not far from the hotel where we were staying. We had planned it that way. But as it is with anything in India, it is one thing to have a plan and quite another as to what hap-

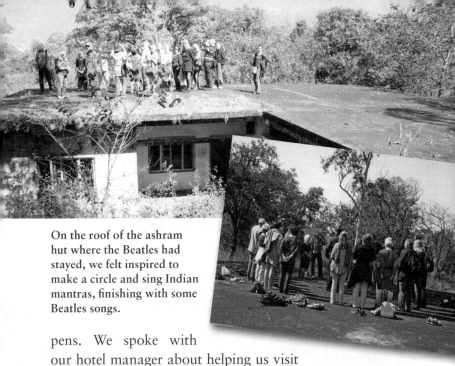

On the roof of the ashram hut where the Beatles had stayed, we felt inspired to make a circle and sing Indian mantras, finishing with some Beatles songs.

pens. We spoke with our hotel manager about helping us visit the ashram since we had heard that it was deserted and locked up. He collected 100 rupees from each of us (the entire Master Class group wanted to go along) which was to be presented to the guard who would un-

We waded off into the bushes again.

Our Master Class in the lecture hall 2014 and the same spot in 1968; the Beatles are sitting on stage with Maharishi.

lock the gate for us.

After we walked in, we had no idea where to start since everything was completely overgrown. The buildings were nearly swallowed by trees, bushes, and branches that have no respect for brick or mortar. We were quite disoriented at first, since in addition to the thick bushes, there were several buildings that had been built after 1970.

Finally we recognized something – it was the house where the Beatles had stayed. Each one of us managed to climb the remains of stairs that led to the roof. Once on top we spontaneously formed a circle and sang some beautiful mantras, finishing with some Beatles' songs.

Then we carefully crawled back down the dilapidated stairs and waded off into the bushes again.

We wanted to find our old rooms and the dining hall, but never succeeded. Then we went looking for the old lecture hall and were ecstatic when we found it! But the state it was in was hard to believe. There were scribbles written all over the moldy surfaces and huge gaping holes in both the walls and ceiling. Bushes were growing inside what remained of the building.

Could this really be the place where we had listened to our guru speak hour upon hour with complete devotion? Somewhere along here I started to share what had happened to me at this place. Originally I thought it would be only Conny and I walking back through the ashram, but our class participants seemed to want to know what had happened here.

The final building on our wish list was Maharishi's villa, and that was the last building we found. We

We are standing on the roof of Maharishi's villa. Without having planned it this way, I shared what had happened between us so long ago. Oops...I started to cry.

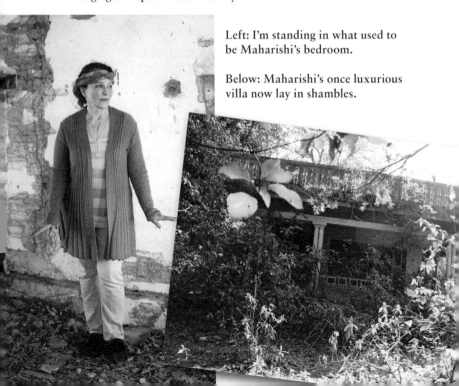

Left: I'm standing in what used to be Maharishi's bedroom.

Below: Maharishi's once luxurious villa now lay in shambles.

would have found it first if we had gone in the other direction when we entered, but for me it was only fitting that the spot filled with the most highly charged memories be saved for last. I found the very spot where I had been sitting by the door of his living room when he first called me out to the garden. Then I found his bedroom, and just like all the others rooms, everything was gone.

The whole place was just an empty shell of crumbling ruins. The last time I was in his villa, there were gorgeous, thick, hand-woven carpets on the floor and the smell of flowers and gentle incense was ever present. There was always a peaceful silence in the atmosphere of his home, and it had felt so special just to be there. We walked up the stairs to the roof, and I found the place where he and I had slept together under the mosquito net with twinkling stars above us on a hot summer night. The tree that I had remembered as being behind us was still there, only larger.

When I began to talk about what had transpired in this once beautiful building, I started to cry. It is that way...if we bring up a memory from the past, all the emotions belonging to that time can come up too if we let them, and these participants were all accustomed to what can happen as we share our deepest thoughts and feelings in a safe setting. At the very end of our long visit, I found a large heart shaped stone as I walked away from the ashram gates and took it with me. It looked ancient and buckled.

We turned to look back at the ashram and happened to notice some other tourists walking through a large hole in the wall that surrounds it. The entire gate opening scenario had been totally unnecessary! Oh well; at least it was nicely symbolic…having the key turned to open the rusty gate of our past.

Later that evening I reflected over the state of this historic ashram. It was not only neglected…it had been vandalized. You'd think that, in view of all the world renown persons who had meditated and created there that the Indian government would renovate the place, at the very least for the sake of tourism. Many asked why Maharishi had abandoned it. What we heard was that the movement never owned the land from the start. It was leased to the Mahesh Yogi Trust in 1961, and paid for by a well-known heiress

I found a heart shaped stone on the ground as I walked away from the ashram. It looked ancient and buckled.

philanthropist named Doris Duke as a favor to her adopted daughter who was one of Maharishi's followers. According to the locals, as the movement became more and more successful, the government raised the cost of the lease. A conflict also arose as to which part of India the ashram belonged, with two states quarreling over ownership. Maharishi got fed up with it all and left, never to return. Perhaps the condition of the ashram is also a kind of statement of the ambivalence surrounding Maharishi's relationship to his home country. He was a famous guru, who had and still has thousands of followers in India, yet there are many who consider him to be too much of a rebel regarding the ancient Hindu traditions of India.

Left on our agenda was to find and re-visit the caves of Tat Wale Baba. Conny had only a vague memory of the actual location, so once again we left it to our hotel manager to be our guide and set off with great expectations. We walked uphill in the foothills of the Himalayas, definitely uphill. We walked, and we walked. The true meaning of foothills really began to sink in after about an hour of treading along this mercilessly leaning path and we finally arrived at what was supposed to be the caves. It was just that they weren't the *right* caves. It turned out that our guide didn't actually know where Tat Wale Baba had been living. Conny was so upset that he felt sick and was convinced the dark forces of the universe had taken over and deliberately misled us.

Another one of our group members, Kiara, was as determined to find the right caves as Conny was upset

Above: We walked up, up into the foothills of the Himalayas.

Left: Approaching the caves of Tat Wale Baba.

Tat Wale Baba: "If you want to become something new, you must completely destroy what you were before." He is about 80 years old in this photo.

and set off on his own to find them, without telling us. The next day he shared in our morning circle that he had managed to retrace our steps and find the spot where we had made a wrong turn. As he walked along the path he now suspected to be the right one, a wild elephant broke through a stone wall in front of him! We had heard about wild elephants in the jungle in this area, but somehow it still seemed like one of those "it won't happen to us" things. Two women who had been in the forest collecting wood recently had been killed by the elephants, so we were duly impressed by Kiara's experience. He said that he had not felt afraid and that the two just looked at each other a moment. Satisfied with what he saw in Kiara, the elephant went on his way, and Kiara moved on ahead up the road. He did find the actual location of the caves but chose not to enter the ashram at that time.

The next day, Conny and two new Indian members of our group who had recently joined us also set off on their own to find the right caves. When they walked by the crossroads where we had made the wrong turn the day before, they asked some local sadhus who were bathing in the mountain river for help. After

Swami Shankardas is the only remaining disciple of Saint Tat Wale Baba.

We listened as the Swami told us how his search for God led him to his master.

being pointed in the right direction, they followed another narrow path climbing up toward the ashram and Conny said he began to feel the divine presence of the saint again as he walked. It was as if he was being taken back in time to the day he first visited the holy Baba.

By this time Kiara had rejoined the group, and all four sat down to perform a Shankaracharya puja Conny had learned at Maharishi's ashram back in 1969. What they didn't expect was that their ceremony would attract the attention of a Swami, who suddenly appeared from the same path they had just walked on. He sat down under the tree where Tat Wale Baba used to sit and teach, and waited respectfully for them to complete the puja. Then introducing himself as Swami

Shankardas, he turned out to be the last living disciple of Tat Wale Baba!

When his master left his body in 1974, he had decided to stay in Rishikesh forever to take care of this simple ashram in the mountain woods. Conny told the Swami of his special visit with Tat Wale Baba and that he and I had become Transcendental Meditation teachers here in Rishikesh with Maharishi. The Swami remembered Maharishi very well, he said.

And so it was that the path was finally open for all of us to visit Tat Wale Baba's caves and get to have

The entrance to TatWale Baba's cave had been locked up since November 2003 by the State Forest Department since the area was declared a national park.

Darshan[10] with his last remaining disciple. I got out my best Punjabi dress and pinned up my hair.

Once seated on the ground around Tat Wale Baba's teaching tree, our whole group spent at least an hour listening to the Swami. He told us that it was his quest to find out who and where God was that eventually led him to a life of service and devotion to his Master. His story was fascinating and genuine. Tat Wale Baba is known as one of the greatest realized yogis of the twentieth century within India but was not known internationally due to the reclusive life that he led in the Himalayas. Those of us who became teachers of meditation with Maharishi in Rishikesh were very fortunate to have met him, and it seems that the two yogis held each other in high esteem.

Tragically and unfathomably, Tat Wale Baba was murdered in 1974 when he was over eighty-five years of age. He was killed by a man who also aspired to become a master and was jealous of this saint's power and reputation. Swami Shankardas had continued to live in the area and look after the ashram all these years. He shared with us that now his life had taken an odd turn. After living the life of a recluse for decades, not participating in society at large, he had been forced by the State Forest Department to close the ashram and leave it in November of 2003. The whole area was to become a national park. He was now studying the law and had become quite an expert on what his legal rights were with regard to whether or not he could be kicked out of Tat Wale Baba's ashram.

---

10  Being in the presence of a highly revered person.

It was a deeply meaningful day and awakened reflections in me of the difference between these two masters. Tat Wale Baba had remained the pure and powerful recluse, staying on track with his focus on the divine through meditation and yoga. He lived a few important principals that someone else had later written down on a piece of parchment placed under "his" tree.

Under the tree where Tat Wale Baba used to meditate lies a parchment with his few simple "thoughts on human life".

Maharishi and Tat Wale Baba 1969.

The baba was not one to travel the world and lecture ... seekers had to travel the world to find him. Maharishi, on the other hand, had walked away from the energy and protection of the Himalayas to bring his teachings to the West and in the process left the recluse part of himself behind. Both men assisted millions of human beings but in different ways. Hindus believe that true yogis and yoginis hold an energy that carries all of mankind, in the same way that we are dependent on the sun for light and warmth. Tat Wale Baba was an outstanding example of that kind of human being. Maharishi, on the other hand, reached millions by spreading a method to help ordinary citizens of the world to find the stillness of a recluse within themselves in the midst of a hectic lifestyle.

**All the other sadhus in the area flocked to Tat Wale Baba's caves and Swami Shankardas to celebrate Shivaratri, a hindu festival celebrating the convergence of Shiva and Shakti, the divine male and female.**

A few months after we left India, we found out that Swami Shankardas' story had a happy end. By a Supreme Court ruling, Shankardas was accepted as a traditional yogi and given the right to stay at the forest ashram to perform yoga and meditation as long as he pleases. Perhaps a reverential visit from thirty western pilgrims had provided an energetic puff in the "right" direction?[11]

Renovated ashram entrance, Judith in lecture hall 2017, and new Beatles graffiti.

11    When the 2015 edition of "Robes..." went to print, a newspaper article from India Today 18/4/15 wrote "Uttarakhand government to use Beatles' Rishikesh visit to revive tourism". I read recently that Maharishi once said to a journalist it was he who made the Beatles famous and not the other way around. And yet it is the 50th anniversary of the Fab Four's time in India that has put a move on some renovation of his old ashram.

The above photos are from our second Master Class trip to India in 2017. The entrance has been renovated enough to charge admission! Well inside, we saw a lot of the brush has been cut back and Maharishi's villa has been cleaned up, but no actual restoration of any of the buildings. Graffiti artists have painted a new Beatles image in the lecture hall that didn't actually exist when they were there, and in the original lecture hall (p. 254) "Let it be" has been painted over the spot where Guru Dev's picture had always been placed and adorned with garlands.

# There is no Santa Claus

I have an old friend who is still in the movement, sort of. She has read my book and tells me that she believes it all. And yet she doesn't tell anyone else about it. In explaining why to me, she said that it would be like having to tell people there is no Santa Claus.

I discovered that there was no Santa Claus when, at the age of six, I looked down at Santa's feet at the family Christmas party and said, "You have the same shoes as Uncle Albert!" I have to admit, though; I wouldn't want to take the initiative to tell a child that there is no Santa. And yet, it sometimes feels like that's what I've done.

Of all the hundreds of letters I have received, not

one has been angry or vindictive. On the other hand, I can't say people haven't been rude towards me about writing the book...it's just that the slander has gone on behind my back. In videos put out on YouTube by members of the TM movement I have been called wacko. In emails to friends and contacts I have been labeled schizophrenic. On TM teacher training courses and on Amazon, I have been described as delusional. I have received international calls and been told I'd better not be lying, otherwise there is some pretty bad karma waiting for me.

Lilou Mace did an interview with me about Robes of Silk when she was in Stockholm during the summer of 2012. She has a popular website with interviews of people who talk about spiritual development, health, ecology, etc. The interview was about twenty minutes long, and I thought it turned out quite well. Her questions were perceptive and to the point. She brought up spiritual leadership and celibacy, the human aspect of someone we regard as divine, and more. Once Lilou had put the video out on her site, a lively dialog ensued with the YouTube link getting about 5000 hits in two weeks. As time went on, the discussion became more and more heated, with the commenters divided into two groups: those who believed me and those who didn't.

Suddenly I received an email from her saying she had taken the video down.

"Your interview is no longer on-line."

She wrote that there were too many negative feelings connected to it, and that the interview had had its consequences.

Several of my readers wrote to Lilou to ask her to put the interview back on-line. She sent another mail explaining that her decision was final. Devout TMers had sent the interview to another journalist to "show what a bad journalist she is". She said she was deeply saddened by this event since her site is about transparency and removing the veil. There were five other interviews on TM on her site (positive ones) with a total of forty five million hits, but she chose to take them all down, since she no longer wanted to have anything to do with TM. The TM story was not her battle, she wrote.

Even though I felt grateful to those who wrote in to defend me, the tone of the comments finally got to a level that sounded like a bunch of squabbling children. Maybe that's the problem...that those of us who found Maharishi at the very beginning of his movement and became deeply devoted to him were looking for some kind of parent figure. I was apparently looking for my beloved grandfather. Conny now sees that his need to follow two gurus for a total of 31 years was the result of a subconscious need to find a father figure he could depend on. Gail Tredwell describes a similar dynamic in her book "Holy Hell". She writes that, at one point during her twenty one years of service to her guru she felt she had found her real mother in Amma, the immensely popular hugging guru. In Maharishi's movement, our dependency on him was more encouraged than discouraged. Many of us saw him as a divine being, myself included. Our Guru became our God. That didn't leave much room for personality traits that were less than perfect. Was he perfect or was it we who needed him to be? For me the search for and subsequent attachment to a divine authority outside of myself has often led down the wrong road...a road filled with greater and greater personal insecurity as to what was right and what was wrong for me, what served my personal growth and what didn't.

From what I hear, Maharishi is not so "worshipped" in the newer waves of teaching meditation, and I think that is good. Of course, we can always be open to learning something helpful from a spiritual teacher, but I find myself getting extremely uncomfortable when, in spiritual circles, where there is too much "devotion" directed toward a spiritual leader. I get this "been there, done that and got the T shirt" feeling. And can still remember the panic that arose once the decision had been made to turn my back on being "devoted" and leave the fold. Would I make it on my own?

In Sweden it is well-known that spring is the time of year to be extra cautious when driving. Young elks have just been kicked out of the family by their mothers who will soon give birth to another calf. The elks which are fully grown have at least some experience with traffic, but the youngsters have just followed their moms around and done as they've been told. All of a sudden, they are alone, without experience, and they are upset and confused enough to present a real danger on the roads, both for themselves and for drivers. Some survive, some don't. There are seven thousand car accidents in Sweden involving elks each year.

From my own experience and from what many of

you have told me in your letters, most of us who were too heavily invested both emotionally and financially with our Guru were like these young abandoned elks when we were either pushed away or chose to leave. As the years had passed we had lost contact with life outside the flock and felt afraid, confused, and depressed. Some of us made it, some didn't. Some were pursued. Some ended up in institutions. Some wrote books. Some actually committed suicide. It seems that those of us who both survived and eventually flourished after "moving out" were those who managed to find support while leaving the fold, either from a new partner, family members, good friends, capable therapists, or organizations that specialize in the study of sects. I have talked with a few who, in spite of working closely with Maharishi, never placed him on a guru pedestal, citing that as the main reason they never went through any kind of separation crisis when it was time to move on.

An important lesson for me has been getting clear on the difference between forgiving and condoning. The experiences you have shared with me have underlined that in spite of his genius at teaching meditation, Maharishi caused a lot of hurt and confusion in many of the women he was intimate with, not to mention all the inner conflicts his "expert" advice created for those who chose a life of celibacy to emulate his spiritual ideals.

Ultimately I think this is a question of whether or not we as devotees are ready to grow up. Part of becoming an "inner" adult is accepting that the parent is not perfect. When my son was sixteen years old, he shared an insight with me. He said, "You know Mom, I always thought all adults were really mature and wise…but now I realize that they aren't." I wish I were as smart as he was when I was sixteen.

Many of you who wrote were both grateful and surprised that my story was not more angry and bitter. But you see I left the flock twice. Once in 1972 when I got on the plane that left Mallorca, and again when I first released the book in 2010. So I had 38 years in between to learn about the traffic. I have vented, processed, questioned and re-evaluated. I had to ask myself why I had needed to follow a guru to begin with and then try to find the guru within. In the end, I had to forgive myself and finally forgive him.

© PeO Larsson

A last word to my Brother and Sister devotees:

My purpose in writing the book was not to try to make you believe me. Long ago, I chose to be co-dependent with Maharishi in agreeing to keep our relationship a secret in spite of his role as a celibate monk and his proclamations that celibacy was the best path for spiritual development. Now I simply want to tell the truth about what I experienced. And when he came to me in a dream to ask for help in cleaning up his karma, I was freed from any distorted sense of obligation to keep covering for him. Now that I have been able to let go of that burden, I feel greatly relieved to have finally taken us both out of the closet. You are free to continue to define him as a divine, faultless being. Another option would be to see that he was a human being who made mistakes and continue to love him as being both human and divine. It's completely up to you.

During the same conversation with my "Santa Claus" friend that I wrote about at the beginning of this chapter, she remembered that Maharishi once said something in front of a Teachers' Training class in the seventies that had made her wonder why he was saying what he was saying:

"You may hear some things about me..." he said. "Just know me in your heart. Know me in your heart."

Judith Bourque was born and raised in the United States. She is an award winning filmmaker and holistic therapist. After graduating from Massachusetts College of Art with a Bachelor's Degree in Fine Arts, she went to India to become a teacher of Transcendental Meditation, and then worked for the TM Movement for two years. She subsequently trained as a teacher of Re-evaluation Counseling, introducing that method to her country of residence, Sweden. She also teaches classes in Dreams as a Source of Spiritual Guidance and Shamanic Healing. After post graduate studies at the Stockholm Academy of Dramatic Arts, she worked at Swedish Television for many years as a film editor, as well as producing and directing independent documentaries. Her films include the "Sowing for Need, or Sowing for Greed?" a documentary on genetically modified seeds, "The Real Patch Adams," and "Hot and Cold Mandala," an experiential infrared film. "Robes of Silk, Feet of Clay" is her first book.